Bong Joon Ho |

Contemporary Film Directors

Edited by Justus Nieland and Jennifer Fay

The Contemporary Film Directors series provides concise, well-written introductions to directors from around the world and from every level of the film industry. Its chief aims are to broaden our awareness of important artists, to give serious critical attention to their work, and to illustrate the variety and vitality of contemporary cinema. Contributors to the series include an array of internationally respected critics and academics. Each volume contains an incisive critical commentary, an informative interview with the director, and a detailed filmography.

For a list of books in the series, please see our website at www.press.uillinois.edu.

Bong Joon Ho |

Joseph Jonghyun Jeon

UNIVERSITY OF
ILLINOIS PRESS
Urbana, Chicago, and Springfield

For Izzi

Contents |

I first became aware of Bong Joon Ho's work in the fall of 2003 at the San Diego Asian Film Festival, for which I happened to be a juror that year. *Memories of Murder (Sarinŭi Ch'uŏk*, 2003) was featured in what would be its US premiere. Just a few years into my first faculty position as a junior professor, I was only beginning as a film scholar. It took me a while to develop a critical apparatus to express my appreciation for the film. It would be nearly a decade before I would publish my thoughts on it, and nearly two decades before I would write my first book on Korean cinema, which includes a pair of chapters focused on Bong's work. What I remember from that evening sitting in the still-darkened theater as the final credits rolled are inchoate feelings of exhilaration and astonishment. I had always enjoyed detective thrillers, but here was a film whose ambitions teemed over the brim of that familiar genre and into a frothier sensorium of historical discontent. Since that night in San Diego, I have followed Bong Joon Ho's career closely, seeing each successive film as soon as it opened and going back to watch earlier work, including the student films at the Korean Film Archive on visits to Seoul in the summers.

So I was intrigued when, in the spring of 2018, over a lovely dinner in Toronto during the Society for Cinema and Media Studies conference that year, the editors of this series asked me to write this book. *Okja* (2017) had just enjoyed a successful run, extending the formidable reputation Bong had built over what was becoming a remarkable career. Still, I thought, it wasn't yet the right time, and I told the editors as much. Though Bong's oeuvre had been impressive to that point, I wanted to see his career complete a culminating arc of some kind before initiating the project. I was confident and hopeful that Bong would continue to make many more films in the next decades, but it wasn't yet clear to me what shape this path would take. I got that culmination sooner than I expected with his very next film, *Parasite* (*Kisaengch'ung*, 2019), which won the Palme d'Or at Cannes and four Oscars at the Academy Awards, including Best Director and Best Picture, the first non-English-language film to win in this last category. At the University of California, Irvine (UCI), where I work, the Center for Critical Korean Studies hosted a pop-up panel on the film a few days after the Oscar triumph, before a packed room. And though some had come for the *jjapaguri* that we served in honor of the film's culinary touch point, the sheer excitement for the film and its tremendous impact were clear in the room. I told the editors that it was time.

For trusting me with this project and for patiently waiting for the right moment, I thank the editors of the Contemporary Film Directors series at the University of Illinois Press, Justus Nieland and Jennifer Fay. They also delivered incredibly useful comments on the original manuscript, for which I am extremely grateful. My experience with the press has been ideal. I received fantastically helpful reader reports from the anonymous reviewers, and editor in chief Danny Nasset, who was also present at that dinner in Toronto, has been a pleasure to work with throughout the process. Mariah Schaefer provided additional support as the book entered production, and Jessica Hinds-Bond supplied superb copyediting. In addition, I am extremely grateful to Bong Joon Ho for agreeing to sit down for the interview that appears in this book and as well to Sharon Choi for providing expert translation services. For setting up the interview, I thank Kyung Hyun Kim, with whom I have had the immense pleasure of coteaching a course on Korean cinema at UCI. I thank the following friends and colleagues for reading drafts of this book and providing a rich intellectual community in which this work could develop: Steve Choe, Chungmoo Choi, Chris Fan, David Fedman, Richard Godden, Oren Izenberg, Laura Kang, Eleana Kim, Se Young Kim, Jerry Lee, Jim Lee, Julia Lee, Nam Lee, Catherine Liu, Ted Martin, Annie McClanahan, Serk Bae Suh, and Michael Szalay.

This work was supported by the Core University Program for Korean Studies of the Ministry of Education of the Republic of Korea and the Korean Studies Promotion Service at the Academy of Korean Studies (AKS-2021-OLU-2250006). Publication of this book was also supported by a grant from the UCI Humanities Center. I thank Judy Wu and Amanda Swain for facilitating this support. Thanks are due as well to Margaret Rhee (University at Buffalo), Hye-Kyoung Kwon (University of North Carolina at Chapel Hill), and Ji-Yeon Jo (University of North Carolina at Chapel Hill) for inviting me to their institutions to present earlier versions of this work. I am also grateful to Suk Koo Rhee for inviting me to teach his graduate students at Yonsei University.

Finally, I want to thank my family. My parents, Sang Joong Jeon and Chung Ja Jeon, have always been loving and supportive. Whatever success I have enjoyed has been the result of their care and persistence. I thank my sister, Christina Cha, for always bringing light and joy into my life. My father-in-law, Choe Jun-Seok, is always a gracious host and fun dinner companion when we visit Korea in the summers. We recently lost my dear mother-in-law, Choe Soon-Nyu. I wish to honor here the memory of her kindness, love, and grace. May she rest in peace. I dedicate this book to my remarkable daughter, Isobel Jeon, who grows each day into a smart, funny, and imaginative person. I can't wait to witness the kind of adult you become, but please do take your time in getting there. Being your father is the greatest honor of my life. Last but not least, this book would not have been possible without the energy and cheer that Youngmin Choe brings me every day (and not just because she is always awake before me to make the coffee). You have always been my biggest fan, and I yours.

A Note on Romanization

Because of the increasing prominence of Koreans in Western public discourse and the range of spellings that we increasingly encounter, Korean proper nouns, including names, are Romanized according to the way in which they are generally presented to English-speaking audiences, by either self-representation, film subtitles, or common usage. The Korean Movie Database (KMDb) was used for the Romanization of names, except in cases where the person has established a presence in Western popular culture with a preferred spelling, as for example with Bong Joon Ho himself. All other Korean words, including film titles, are Romanized according to the McCune-Reischauer system.

Global Entanglements |

In the denouement of Bong Joon Ho's 2009 crime drama *Mother* (*Madŏ*), knots only become more tangled. The film's eponymous and unnamed mother (Kim Hye-ja) visits the man who has been imprisoned for her son's crime. Learning that the wrongfully accused prisoner is mentally disabled like her son, she is racked with guilt. She realizes that her unconditional love has made her blind to her son's shortcomings. The murder her son committed has, furthermore, led to one of her own, the killing of an indigent man who witnessed the original crime. As the mother is faced with the repercussions of her actions in the jail, individual consciousness confronts the prospect of social responsibility. Should she reveal the truth or protect her son (and herself)? Reckoning with her hypocrisy, she is tortured by the demand for justice that she herself has loudly trumpeted throughout the film, even in the face of derision by the small-town community. But though she is forced to reckon with her own violence, deception, and injustice, she experiences this reckoning as internal anguish rather than as juridical punishment.

Ultimately, she remains firm in her resolve to hide the truth. While her private torment is expressed in a public institution, a state-operated incarceration center, she desperately endeavors to prevent the entanglement of these two realms of experience. She chooses to protect her son.

Over the course of Bong Joon Ho's career, the entanglements become larger, more intricate, and harder to disavow. *Mother* is a pivotal film in his oeuvre, which moves in a general trajectory from a point of view firmly situated in a rapidly modernizing South Korea toward an increasingly global orientation. To borrow James Tweedie's description of global New Wave cinemas, Bong's films increasingly become "at once a product and an account of globalization . . . a record of the disruption that follows in the wake of socioeconomic upheaval" (20). Indeed, it is in part their own escalating status as successful global products that gives Bong's films purchase for their insights into globalization. The trajectory, however, is incremental, building toward complexity on more foundational insights. In the mother's jail-scene torment, the narrow bounds of private consciousness confront wider social implications, indexing the gradual broadening of scale that one witnesses over the course of Bong's films. Here, the mother's narrow interests come in conflict with those of her community. Her initial desire to prioritize the well-being of her disabled son proves to be impossible without profound fallout. Even as both she and her son get away with murder, her uneasy ambivalence in the final scene of the film—when she dances on a bus full of people on a fun excursion to hide the fact of her guilt (figure 1)—ultimately signals the inevitability of social entanglements. She had practiced the dancing alone in a field earlier, but even while rehearsing in private, she was thinking about the perceptions of others. Like the bus in this final scene, the world she lives in is crowded.

The historical backdrop for Bong Joon Ho's cinematic imagination is indeed a crowded world, namely the US-led wave of globalization begun near the end of the twentieth century, which had a tremendous impact not just on the world's economy but also on social life in once more discrete locales. The large-scale circulation of commodities and capital that it comprised, however, did not so much produce a homogenous global culture as create cacophony. Emerging at precisely this confusing historical moment, the films of Bong Joon Ho explored with great urgency the dynamics of globalization and the modernization processes that led into

Figure 1. The mother dancing on a crowded bus
excursion at the end of *Mother*.

it. But his films offer piercing examinations of the global circuits of the twenty-first century not just because they take on a wide view but also paradoxically because they remain rooted in idiosyncratic experiences. For Bong Joon Ho such experiences are Korean experiences. From this situated perspective, Bong Joon Ho's films at first surveyed the fallout from South Korea's rapid modernization and then moved on to consider how these more localized dynamics reverberated in global geographies and how the large-scale movements of power and capital redounded back on the lives of people preoccupied with the vicissitudes of everyday life. Because of this divided focus, Bong Joon Ho's films have pulled in contrary directions throughout his entire career, toward the tiniest of details on the one hand and toward convoluted, far-reaching systems on the other. As a result, his cinematic imagination remains grounded and concrete even when the view is capacious and refractive.

Bong Joon Ho's career began with a series of films generally focused on the entanglements of *modernization*. These films articulated the discontents of modern Korea from a highly localized perspective that became globally infiltrated, primarily by US hegemonic power as a crucial accelerator of Korean modernity. After this early period, he turned to a series of films generally focused on the entanglements of *globalization*. In a turn made possible by early success both at international film festivals and at the box office, these later films were more expansively situated and aimed more toward global audiences, often featuring iconic Western actors—like Chris Evans, Tilda Swinton, and

Robert Pattinson—speaking in English. *Mother* subtly marks this larger pivot through the mother's tormented acknowledgment of the broader social relations that her own interests must necessarily repress, the fact that her actions have consequences for others. As a result, the film helps us appreciate the tension in Bong's oeuvre that complicates abstract concepts like modernization and globalization, which are ultimately part of the same historical process. The intense scrutiny of such concepts is a major preoccupation of Bong Joon Ho's work.

The mise-en-scène of the jail scene expresses the mother's torment, calling our attention to the mundane particularity of this small-town jail, where this extraordinary crime promises to become misremembered, as a wrongfully accused man disappears into an institutional abyss. Literally meaning *putting or placing onstage or in scene*, mise-en-scène gives weight to idiosyncratic particularity, providing texture to the world invoked in the artwork by specifying milieu. A concept derived from theater, mise-en-scène in cinema includes "all the elements that together shape the interaction between beings and objects before the camera" (Tweedie 51). The small-town setting of *Mother*, with its provincial prejudices, deeply informs the intense claustrophobia experienced by characters in the diegesis and as well by the audience. The mise-en-scène is part of the film's studious effort to capture the gritty feel of its decidedly uncosmopolitan setting, where small-town cops accustomed to policing more prosaic offenses struggle to solve an unusual murder.

Without exception, Bong Joon Ho's films foreground mise-en-scène as part of a fastidious preoccupation with the spaces they depict, whether a Korean apartment building, a small town in the countryside, a futuristic train that navigates the icy terrain of a postapocalyptic world, or a posh house in an exclusive Seoul neighborhood. Such distinctively textured settings offer more than rich visual backgrounds; they also drive the plots of the stories by encompassing the imaginary worlds depicted in each film. Yun-ju (Lee Sung-jae) is oppressed by the proximity of his neighbors in *Barking Dogs Never Bite* (*P'ŭllandasŭŭi kae*, 2000), epitomized by the yappy barking of a woman's dog, which becomes a figure of his frustrations over his stalled career. The naive backwater town in *Memories of Murder* (*Sarinŭi Ch'uŏk*, 2003) thrown into chaos by a serial killer reflects the tension between tradition and modernity that aggravates the sensorium of the film. For the residents of Wilford's (Ed

Harris) train in *Snowpiercer* (*Sŏlgukyŏlch'a*, 2013), there is no possibility for life outside of the train, and thus they struggle for control over it. Underneath the ritzy house in *Parasite* (*Kisaengch'ung*, 2019) is a bleak bunker built for surviving North Korean missile attacks and escaping creditors, but even the house's owners are unaware of it. In all these examples, a fully realized mise-en-scène frames the central conceptual concerns that motivate character action and organize plot.

We might think of Bong Joon Ho's fashioning of mise-en-scène in relation to the way in which postwar filmmakers and critics in the French New Wave found in it a strategy for scaling down classical Hollywood's commercial project and for signaling a distinctive auteurist vision, by introducing contingency, chance, and particularity to an art form that had become too committed to highly mannered sets (Tweedie 53). In bustling Parisian urbanscapes, French New Wave directors found antidotes to cinema as defined by dominant American studios. At the same time, this mode of filmmaking and of criticism revealed itself almost immediately to be overdetermined by US cultural hegemony in Europe following World War II under the Marshall Plan. Thus, even in these French articulations of mise-en-scène, we could witness "the emergence of an American-style modernity organized around consumption and the market—manifested not through grand ideological statements but through a pervasive, commonplace, and over time almost pedestrian transformation of everyday life" (Tweedie 52). So, while it seemed to attractively foreground the local and particular, mise-en-scène was revealed to be already entangled in broader systems of exchange and political economy. Even with the auteurist pretensions of the French New Wave, mise-en-scène straddled a fundamental contradiction, expressing at once the director's vision and "the defiant otherness of the material world recorded by the filmmaker" (Tweedie 27). Bong Joon Ho is famous for his meticulous approach to filmmaking, for his detailed storyboards for each film and the idiosyncratic details (dubbed *Bong-tails* by admirers) captured in his shots. But if there is auteurism in Bong Joon Ho's work, it appears less as transcendent agency and more as a site for encountering, as Timothy Corrigan put it in his essay "The Commerce of Auteurism," "the different conditions through which expressive meaning is made by an auteur and reconstructed by an audience, conditions which involve historical and cultural motivations and rationalizations" (48; see

Figure 2. The mother facing the falsely accused
man in *Mother*.

also Sung). As for many canny filmmakers from the French New Wave on, mise-en-scène helps Bong Joon Ho express one's embeddedness within larger frameworks of determination.

The jail scene expresses this sense of embeddedness through its mise-en-scène. Here, a sequence of shots encapsulates the vexed pivot between personal interest and social responsibility that implies incremental movement toward larger determining frames. The falsely accused man is led into the room, wearing drab prison garb that visually echoes the gray institutional walls, a blending that is emphasized by the initially out-of-focus camera before he sits down to face the mother through a clear plexiglass partition, which we only notice because of the holes to allow for conversation. The scene then depicts the brief conversation between them in shot-reverse-shot format, with the sturdy torso of the detective—hands in his pockets and his gray blazer open showing his belt buckle—visible over the mother's shoulder (figure 2). The mother of the real killer begins to cry and lowers her head as the man tries to comfort her. The mise-en-scène in this sequence functions in a similar manner to Robert Bresson's use of jail cells in Susan Sontag's account: to manifest a character's interior conflict, "the fight against oneself" (130). But rather than use the space of incarceration solely to suggest the torturous confinements of subjective interiority, Bong's jail scene also expresses the irrepressible fact of social entanglement, which threatens the desire to preserve unbothered autonomy.

To emphasize this challenge to solitary consciousness, the next shot shows the characters through a series of glass partitions from the perspective of a room several units away, as the prisoner is led out of the facility (which was designed to accommodate several simultaneous prisoner visits), as if to reach for a removed perspective (figure 3). The partition openings appear smaller as they recede toward the room where the mother sits; and so, the scene looks for a moment like a particular form of mise en abyme, in which the image in a mirror facing another mirror produces the visual effect of infinite reflection, as is remembered, for example, in Orson Welles's iconic shot from *Citizen Kane* (1941). Here, we see the endless reflections of Charles Foster Kane (Welles) walking through a room with mirrors on either side of him (figure 4). In *Mother*, such a staging reflects the mother's mental state, her awareness of her own guilt and that of her son, with the reverberations of her guilt becoming manifest in the visual echoes of the panoptic mise en abyme. After a beat, however, we see that we have been mistaken. These are windows, not mirrors. We note the varied position of the chairs in each room and the way that the image of the characters themselves is not reflected. Nevertheless, a version of the initial implication holds. Instead of an endless duplication of an identical scene, the shot instead offers us a series of similar examples. Instead of iteration, we are given relation. Even if the mother herself refuses to acknowledge social responsibility, its apparatus become literalized around her.

Mise en abyme of course encompasses a broader aesthetic category than the Wellesian visual trick. By self-reflexively indexing a work of art's internal logic, as André Gide described (30–31), mise en abyme

Figure 3. View of the mother through a series of partitions as the falsely accused man is led away in *Mother*.

Figure 4. Visual mise en abyme in *Citizen Kane.*

generally suggests the relation between larger extradiegetic structures, frameworks, and phenomena and their smaller diegetic counterparts. In so doing, mise en abyme offers an opportunity for an artwork to reflect on its own conceits as if from an external perspective, as in the moment in *Memories of Murder* when the detectives take a break from their brutal interrogation to eat lunch and watch, comically along with the suspect, a popular television police procedural called *Inspector Chief.* In this instance, the film playfully reveals its own generic orientation while foregrounding its departures. Classically figured as the proverbial play within a play, mise en abyme in film most often appears in movies that are about moviemaking, featuring representations of behind-the-scenes dynamics among the cast and crew (as in Kim Chang-rae's independent film *Let Me Out* [*Ren mi aut*, 2013]) or of dealmaking by industry executives (as in Robert Altman's *The Player* [1992]). Bong Joon Ho's work delivers a handful of explicit moments in this self-reflexive mode—Lucy Mirando's orchestration of a media spectacle in *Okja* (*Okcha*, 2017), or the Kim family's rehearsal of their roles like actors in their long con of the Park family in *Parasite.* More often however in Bong's work, mise en abyme appears in more subtle forms, through which a film might reflect on the film's own apparatus—like the scene in *Memories of Murder* when Detective Seo in a darkened room holds up a flashlight while flipping through series of photographs pertaining to the case, as if to re-create the mechanics of film image projection.

Through such self-reflexive tactics, mise en abyme alerts us to our immersion in broader systemic relations by offering occasions for comparison, even if those relations sometimes prove to be projective illusions. The version exemplified by the Welles shot literalizes the self-reflexive reflection that characterizes the broader aesthetic by showing how mise en abyme operates paradoxically: pictorial (or representational) space seems to expand in breadth in ever-receding reflections, but at the same time this spatial expansion is recognized as fictive and thus accompanied by a different sort of claustrophobia. Endless copies direct our attention outward while questioning whether this expanded scale offers real alternatives. In *Mother*'s jail scene, the invocation of mise en abyme, a site of both insight and disorientation, suggests the magnitude of the mother's cover-up, its cascading ripple effects. She realizes that hers is not a victimless crime but rather one that has inflicted significant harm on innocent bystanders. It is a crime that echoes into adjacent spaces, not an isolated action but one that resounds with larger social consequences.

We see a similar use of mise en abyme within the provocatively delimited mise-en-scène of the futuristic train in Bong's 2013 sci-fi thriller *Snowpiercer*, Bong's next film after *Mother*. Near the beginning of the story, we see Curtis (Chris Evans) standing with his eyes fixed forward, ignoring the guard's order to sit down. However, what initially seems like an act of intransigence is revealed to be a tactic in a practical scheme. Curtis is not staring at the guard in defiance but rather looking beyond him and through the open door of the train car ahead, timing how long the doors that divide the cars stay open in an attempt to gain intelligence for a future rebellion. As the camera reverses from a shot of Curtis standing to a view through the open doors, we see mise en abyme in the object of Curtis's forward gaze. Here the invocation blends the visual logic of Welles's camera trickery with Gide's formulation, in which mise en abyme points toward the artwork's internal structure. Indeed, in *Snowpiercer*, the long-concatenated structure of the train is identical to the film's episodic narrative structure: to move through the various cars of the train as Curtis's rebel band manages to do during the film is to advance the film's plot, each open door beginning a new episode or sequence. The basic structuring principle of Wilford's wondrous train—which carries the entirety of the earth's remaining survivors after an environmental disaster has wiped out the planet's population—is that everyone has a specific place, a place that happens to correspond to class difference, with the poor in the tail and the wealthy up front. As the rebels proceed through the train cars and accumulate experiences, their perspective of the whole train becomes more complete, but the knowledge accrued in this process turns out to be unsatisfying. The once-idealized head of the train disappoints. Accordingly, having passed from tail to engine, Curtis gradually seems to obtain the kind of disconcerting big-picture knowledge that tormented the mother in the other scene. He learns that what he thought was a revolution to upend the train's social hierarchy was really a plot to perpetuate it, with Curtis himself taking over as the new conductor. Both Curtis and the mother move from the blinkered concerns of individual preoccupations to an appreciation of social totality, the full picture of which ultimately simply reproduces the smaller-scale confinements, like the ever-receding reflections in *Citizen Kane*.

Mise-en-scène and mise en abyme are of course neither discreet nor oppositional aesthetic categories in film art. A scene's mise-en-scène might well contain elements that self-reflexively indicate the film's aware-ness of itself as film, just as mise en abyme is often tied to the particular-ity of its setting. Rather, each refers to specific techniques of placement, implying distinctive strategies of spatial articulation, that open onto and elaborate social relations. So, instead of simply reducing mise-en-scène to local particularity and mise en abyme to global scale, I want to think of each as formal tools that become intertwined in Bong's work for articulating spatial cartographies and for correlating filmic space to broader geographies. In working between mise-en-scène and mise en abyme, the historiographic method of this book suggests a revisionist approach to auteurism that builds on Corrigan's emphasis on commerce and celebrity, oriented now at a wider scale toward its systematic and political-economic entanglements. And though it is concerned with the work of a single and highly successful director (and published in a book series organized around the same logic), this book is thus inspired by and builds on the work of film scholars like Jerome Christensen in

America's Corporate Art (2011), J. D. Connor in *The Studio after the Studios* (2015), and Jeff Menne in *Post-Fordist Cinema* (2019), who have conceptually foregrounded the Hollywood studio as a corporate institution to complicate and undercut naive celebrations of auteurial agency. Though less interested in the studio/firm as the site of agential determination, this book shares with this body of work a concern for the way in which economic conditions and pressures become primary frameworks for cinematic production. Alongside these studies focused on Hollywood industry analysis, this book also builds on media industries work within Korean media studies, which foregrounds the material conditions in which Korean film has emerged. This subfield includes the work of Chi-Yun Shin and Julian Stringer in *New Korean Cinema* (2005), Jinhee Choi in *The South Korean Film Renaissance* (2010), Hye Seung Chung and David Scott Diffrient in *Movie Migrations* (2015), Brian Yecies and Aegyung Shim in *The Changing Face of Korean Cinema, 1960 to 2015* (2016), Dal Yong Jin in *Transnational Korean Cinema* (2019), and Sangjoon Lee in *Cinema and the Cultural Cold War* (2020).

A key issue for the transnational Korean milieu in which Bong Joon Ho has made his films, a distinction more of degree than of kind, is the role of the international distribution market relative to the domestic box office for filmmakers like Bong who work from a national context but with hopes to transcend it. Bong's earlier films built their success on strong domestic ticket sales. Of its $89 million in worldwide receipts, for example, *The Host* (*Koemul*, 2006) grossed just under $65 million of that amount at the South Korean box office. But as the films sought wider global audiences, the proportions became more skewed. *Parasite*, for example, grossed just over $70 million in South Korea versus just over $258 million worldwide ("Parasite"). Although Hollywood has become increasingly dependent on global box office receipts, the ratios have rarely been so drastic. Beyond the box office, filmmakers working outside of the Hollywood framework like Bong have become more reliant on international film festivals to guarantee success, and in many cases even to guarantee success in the domestic market. All this means that filmmaking in this context must necessarily conceive of itself at least in some respect as an export venture, even as innovative directors have wished, as was the case for the French New Wave, to foreground local particularity.

In the context of these production and distribution realities, the use of mise-en-scène and mise en abyme that I have been tracking so far in Bong Joon Ho's films might be regarded as strategies for articulating in film art what political theorists have described as *combined and uneven development*. Originally articulated by Leon Trotsky and further elaborated in the academic field of geography (where the concept is often shortened to "uneven development"), its logic, as Neil Smith puts it, "derives specifically from the opposed tendencies, inherent in capital, toward the differentiation but simultaneous equalization of the level and the conditions of production" (6). Because capitalist economies develop unevenly in different locations, capital can be moved from one location to another to seek higher rates of profit and lower labor costs, particularly at historical moments when powerful governments and corporations prioritize the building and maintaining of globalized trade networks. This means that individual nations tend toward integration into larger global systems that orchestrate what otherwise might be experienced as discrete phenomena. Such transnational economic arrangements in turn also have transformative social consequences. According to Smith, combined and uneven development "is social inequality blazoned into the geographical landscape, and it is simultaneously the exploitation of that geographical unevenness for certain socially determined ends" (206). The concept is an incitement to think globally about local social relations and about the operations of capital in and across broader ecologies.

In Bong's work, then, mise-en-scène and mise en abyme become tools for formally articulating the spatial paradoxes and contradictions that emerge under such global regimes. They become, in essence, tools for charting the expansion of capital relations in globalization and the social reorganization it demands. When viewed from a remove, such massive global systems can be daunting to understand, but Bong's conceptual toolbox helps make sense of the mess. To return to the two shots from the jail scene in *Mother*: mise-en-scène suggests the *place of entanglement* within a particular set of circumstances, while mise en abyme suggests the *scale of entanglement* with a broader system of relations. Mise-en-scène indexes the particularity of a certain space understood in localized terms while at the same time considering how that local space might be externally determined. Mise en abyme indexes the relation of this space to others like it in other places, even as it worries that capital has the capacity to simply reproduce its dynamics no matter the location. Such tools become necessary because the world for which they are fashioned is an increasingly disorienting one. Bong Joon Ho's films work to temper this disorientation by patiently mapping out what coordinates might be ascertained despite the chaos.

In the face of such disorientation, a pressing question becomes, *where are we?* Not coincidentally, this question recurs throughout Bong Joon Ho's oeuvre. It is the question that the big-city detective, Seo (Kim Sang-kyung), seems to ask himself when he arrives in the small town in *Memories of Murder*. It is implicit on the faces of Curtis's band of rebels as they move through the wonders of each successive compartment on Wilford's train. Dr. Johnny Wilcox's (Jake Gyllenhaal) disorientation at Mija's (Ahn Seo-hyun) mountaintop home in Korea is matched by Mija's feeling of dislocation when she arrives in New York City to rescue her pet pig. Chung-sook (Jang Hye-jin) fails to conceal her astonishment when the housekeeper she has replaced shows her the gothic basement underneath the Parks' fancy house in *Parasite*.

In these and many other cases in Bong's films, this sense of spatial disorientation is simultaneously also one of temporal dislocation: *when are we?* A figure of modern scientific method, Seo is dismayed by the backward investigative techniques of the local detectives, who are unaware of new techniques. Curtis and his friends are given a quick introduction to the future-oriented vision that informs all operations on the train, as that vision is indoctrinated into the minds of young children in the school car scene through the recounting of a history of the enterprise that produced their moving community. Dr. Wilcox is both confounded by the lack of creature comforts at Mija's house and impressed by the fact that old-world animal husbandry methods, very different from the high-tech operations of the Mirando Corporation, yielded such a miraculous specimen. Chung-sook's descent into the basement bunker figures the way in which modern Korea always rests on the foundation (literally in this case) of its traumatic war-torn past.

The experience of such dislocations, spatial and temporal, were formative for Bong both during his childhood and throughout his career as a filmmaker. Bong Joon Ho was born on September 14, 1969, in the South Korean city of Daegu. Although the third-largest city in the nation at the time, it was considered a provincial location, not dissimilar to the small-town milieu depicted in *Mother*. Despite this decidedly uncosmopolitan setting, Bong's was a family of intellectuals. Bong's father, Bong Sang-gyun, was a graphic designer and professor of art. Bong's two siblings went on to become professors at prominent universities in Seoul. His maternal grandfather is the writer Park Tae-won, an important literary figure who wrote about the Japanese colonial period in Korea before defecting to North Korea during the Korean War. This decision caused his family remaining in South Korea, including Bong Joon Ho's mother, Park So-young, a good deal of difficulty. It was trying for the family during the Cold War, which was particularly tense on the divided Korean peninsula after the Korean War; and this tension remained a pervasive characteristic of Korean life long after the fall of the Berlin Wall and the end of the Cold War in the West.

When Bong Joon Ho was in elementary school, his family moved to Seoul, and specifically to the Jamsil neighborhood on the east side of the city, just south of the Han River, which divides the older parts of Seoul to the north from the newer neighborhoods to the south. This was a time of rapid modernization, and Jamsil was an ideal location from which to view this societal transformation. Coming from a far more provincial location at an age when he was old enough to register the differences, Bong was afforded the kind of comparative perspective that Raymond Williams describes in *The Country and the City*, from which one can perceive a broader social change because the older and new ways of life for a certain generation coexist at the same time and place (37). Bong developed the ability to speak Korean in both Daegu and Seoul dialects and would regularly alternate between them at home and at school (J. Jung 178–79). Indeed, making virtue out of dislocation, this linguistic and, ultimately, perspectival promiscuity became the foundation for much of Bong's filmmaking, which can move fluidly between localized orientations and cosmopolitan sensibilities.

During his childhood after moving to Seoul, Bong witnessed hasty urbanization, most prominently in the construction of massive apartment complexes, which sprouted up in his neighborhood of Jamsil just as they did in many locations around the city. The mise-en-scène of Bong's first film, *Barking Dogs Never Bite*, focused on one of these apartment complexes, along with their modernizing implications. Jamsil was also a primary site for the 1988 Olympic Games in Seoul, which constituted a watershed moment for South Korean development, marking the entrance of the once poverty-stricken nation onto the global stage. Much of Bong's early work focuses on this period of rapid transition, which sociologist Chang Kyung-sup termed *compressed modernity*. The year 1988 also marked the end of the military dictatorship in South Korea and the beginning of democracy after years of struggle.[1] Coming from a family that harbored a great deal of animosity toward the military dictatorship in South Korea—Bong's father was a particularly strenuous detractor—Bong obtained a social consciousness from a relatively young age. Growing up Catholic at a time when the Catholic Church in South Korea was active in the democracy movement, Bong was made aware of the pressing social issues of the day (J. Jung 186–87). He also participated in protests against the authoritarian government, some of which erupted in violence. He was even jailed for a month for joining a teachers union demonstration (Rayns).

Bong began as a college student in 1988, that pivotal year in South Korean history, attending Yonsei University, considered one of the best universities in South Korea, where he majored in sociology. Although he chose a more traditional academic discipline over something in the arts, Bong had been interested in becoming a film director from a young age, having spent much of his childhood watching movies on his family's television set, including the Hollywood movies that were broadcast on the Armed Forces Korea Network (AFKN), a US Army station broadcast out of the US military base in Seoul (J. Jung 182). While a university student, Bong started a film club called the Yellow Door, named after the color of the door in the room where the group met. Through this club, Bong gained his first real experiences in film production. Aside for an unreleased short seen only by a handful of friends, his first student film was a short entitled *White Man* (*Paeksaekin*, 1994). After completing his compulsory military service and graduating from Yonsei, Bong enrolled in the Korean Academy of Film Arts (KAFA), an important film school in South Korea, which has produced several prominent Korean film directors. His graduation film at KAFA was *Incoherence* (*Chilimyŏllyŏl*, 1994), a three-part short film about the hypocrisy of a series of prominent men in Korean society.

Incoherence received a good deal of buzz at festivals, particularly for a student work, drawing the attention of director Park Chan-wook. Bong nevertheless initially struggled to get a foothold in the famously hierarchical system of Chungmuro (the equivalent of Hollywood in South Korea), in which Korean directors typically endured long apprenticeships before being entrusted with their own projects. He eventually met influential producer Cha Seung-jae, who would produce Bong's first two feature films. Bong was fortunate to arrive at a moment when the Korean film industry, like much of Korean culture in general, was undergoing a profound transformation, particularly with the influx of new capital, first from *chaebol* (the historical family-owned conglomerates that played a central role in Korea's economic development in the second half of the twentieth century) and then from other more risk-tolerant corporate sources that emerged in the period to take advantage of new opportunities. Beginning with the historic success of *Shiri* (1999), a domestic film that broke Korean box office records formerly set by Hollywood blockbusters like *Titanic* (1997), the new conditions led to a production boom that loosened the grip of Chungmuro's old hierarchical system, giving young directors like Bong opportunities that they might have had to wait for in earlier decades.

Delivering his first feature at the turn of the century, Bong in his work examines a moment of multivalent transition. His films follow on the heels of the so-called Korean New Wave directors—including Lee Chang-dong (*Peppermint Candy* [*Pakha Satang*, 1999]), Jang Sun-woo (*The Age of Success* [*Sŏnggongsidae*, 1988]), and Park Kwang-su (*Chilsu and Mansu* [*Ch'ilsuwa Mansu*, 1988])—whose films grappled with the vertiginous social and political transformations of the 1980s, moving from a period of protest and violence toward the end of authoritarian rule. Emerging at the end of South Korea's period of compressed modernity, New Wave directors were particularly concerned with processing historical trauma and grappling with a tumultuous past (K. H. Kim, *Remasculinization* 27–30; J. Choi 166–73). Bong's childhood did indeed correspond with this period, but his work speaks more properly to the historical period immediately following, when rapid growth began to slow and when Koreans came to realize that the dramatic economic expansion of the previous generation had also caused a good deal of unanticipated negative consequences. A watershed moment for this turn was the 1997–98 Asian financial crisis. Known in Korea as the International Monetary Fund (IMF) crisis, it began as a liquidity problem when the pervasive international short-term loans that had been driving economic activity quickly dried up amid extreme currency fluctuations (J. J. Jeon, *Vicious* 1–26). As serious as these initial events may have been, however, the greatest legacy of the crisis was the terms of the IMF bailout itself, which instead of seeking to simply stabilize the economy according to the historical charge of the Bretton Woods institution instead forced a draconian restructuring of the South Korean economy following Western models and to the benefit of Western capital. Here was a familiar cocktail that had become globally prominent during the Washington Consensus, the US-centric world economic system that emerged in the 1990s and that culminated with the forming of the World Trade Organization in 1995. Part of the Washington Consensus apparatus, the IMF generally encouraged the privatization of public resources, loosening of protectionist trade policies, and weakening of labor protections. In a move that was orchestrated by powerful figures in the US Department of the Treasury (with ties to Wall Street banking), the IMF in this instance imposed structural changes in an interventionist spirit that would fundamentally alter the course of South Korean economic and social life in the decades to come, which would be characterized by rising inequality, increasingly precarious labor conditions, and skyrocketing rates of household debt. From the vantage point of the present, we can see that these changes were permanent.

In addition to measures designed to give corporations more freedom and leverage, particularly against organized labor, the intervention of the US Treasury through the vehicle of the IMF under the banner of Washington Consensus free trade ideology gave significantly greater access for foreign capital to Korean businesses, which had historically been shielded by the developmental state's protectionist policies. In the motion picture industry, for instance, the quota system that had protected domestic producers from Hollywood dominance was significantly weakened during this period (J. Choi 3). As it had in many places throughout the world from Latin America to Asia, the IMF structural adjustment functioned in part as a more polite (if coldly clinical) update to gunboat diplomacy, a subtler strategy for opening up protected economies that replaced traditional forms of colonial aggression with neocolonial asymmetrical trading networks, which were themselves designed as spatial fixes for slowing growth in deindustrializing Western economies. South Korea in this context is then an exemplary figure for a global transformation that was ultimately orchestrated by a US hegemony in decline. An important US ally in Asia (one of the few nations, for example, to send troops to the United States' more unpopular wars, in Vietnam and Iraq), South Korea gave the United States a military, economic, and cultural stronghold in Asia—a place from which to check, first, Japan's threat to global dominance in the 1980s and then, later, that of China at the turn of the millennium—often using the old Cold War animosity with North Korea as cover for these motives.

Regarding Korean history, the idea of *compressed modernity* is too often cited either under the rubric of national pride (that South Korea was able to accomplish in the space of a few decades what took much longer in other developing countries) or else in relation to the bewildering effects of modernization. But coining the term in 1999, just a year before the release of Bong's first film, sociologist Chang Kyung-sup argued that compressed modernity encompassed not just rapid economic development and cognitive disorientation over its pace but also, as was becoming clear after the IMF crisis, a profound concern about sustainability: "A most unnerving realization in this regard is that what they have built up in such a hurry turns out to be a highly collapse-prone economic, political and social system." Crucially, Chang's insight was not merely that such rapid expansions inevitably come to an end but, more radically, that they are self-canceling, "that the very mechanisms and strategies for achieving rapid national development now function as fundamental obstacles to current and future development" ("Compressed" 31).

We might employ this fuller accounting of Chang's influential concept in turn to clarify the now well-trodden periodization problem among Korean film historians about how to distinguish the so-called Korean New Wave from New Korean Cinema. Shin and Stringer asked in 2005, "Upon invoking the name 'New Korean Cinema,' when exactly do we mean?" (5). While scholars had identified a New Wave in films made between the mid-1980s and the mid-1990s, others had identified continuities with later filmmaking, leading to the term New Korean Cinema as a larger, catchall category. In 2010, Jinhee Choi remained resolute in declaring that "current attempts to define the starting point of the New Korean cinema are unsatisfactory," since "the precise referent of the Korean New Wave shifts from author to author" (6). Such debates are perhaps more important to argue than to settle, but the fuller account of Chang's *compressed modernity* offered above suggests a conceptual frame in which the Korean New Wave and New Korean Cinema might be regarded as both discreet and overlapping periodizing categories, as two sides of the same coin: one focusing on Korean compressed modernity and its discontents (the traumatic legacy of colonialism and war, the struggle for democratization, and the transformation of traditional Korean life), and the other focusing on the late capitalist revelation that the mechanisms of early growth are the same that now propel stagnation.

Though poised firmly in the later period category by virtue of release dates, Bong Joon Ho's films remain bound to the past from which they emerge. If a primary task for the Korean New Wave was to express the traumatic burdens of the past, the historical task for Bong (following Chang's insight about the ultimately symbiotic relationship between modernity's expansion and its subsequent decline) is to question our understandings of the past and the various possibilities for the future to which those understandings lead. Invariably situated within a global history, Korean history becomes less a movement from a heroic industrial development (the Miracle on the Han) to a debased neoliberal present and more a short-term bargain with ineluctable long-term consequences. At this specific historical moment, then, Bong's cinema attempts to re-evaluate the complicated dynamics of this transition at various scales, connecting individual experience to national imaginaries to geopolitical undercurrents. It is no accident that his first two films (*Barking Dogs Never Bite* and *Memories of Murder*) are crime dramas that attempt to ascertain guilt, each within a highly localized mise-en-scène that occasions reflection on the costs of modernity. Both films play on Raymond Williams's comparative frame—the simultaneous copresence of the country and the city, in which past forms persistently reappear even as the way of life they represent vanishes—to interrogate Korean modernization processes (Chang, "Compressed" 35–37). In these early films, we witness the kind of uneven transformations that characterize these processes. *Barking Dogs Never Bite* offers the apartment complex as the site of this change, while *Memories of Murder* worries about the problem of a modern crime (serial killing) in a formerly innocent small town.

Furthermore, for both Bong and Williams, this transition repeats itself on a global scale in the relationship between colony and metropole, complicating questions of local modernity with those of imperialist logics that persist long after the age of formal colonization (Williams 279–88). In thinking through such global transnational relations in Bong's work, one important point of scholarly emphasis has been on his playful use of genre (N. Lee, *Films* 40–42). Many of his films have indeed been heralded for their ability to deploy genre in a way that adapts given forms for the South Korean context and demonstrates the dynamics of geopolitical relations. The term *genre-bending* has frequently been used in such discussions to describe this process of appropriation and adaptation. But while such accounts are useful, they tend to understate the way in which genres by their very nature are inherently always in flux, even as they appear to have stabilized into an established tradition. Genre is an ever-changing phenomenon in which forms of contingency—be they historical, regional, or aesthetic—seem to stabilize into a coherent formation. Theodore Martin has described genre as formal features of a given artwork that *sediment* over time (6–8). The geological metaphor is appropriate: sediment is at once the product of dynamic variable forces (movement of water, weight of rock, temperature of earth, etc.) and at the same time a hardened form that obtains a permanent quality. Sediment is often layered, offering a motionless record of the temporal processes that created it. As such it preserves not only the physical material that composes it but also a sense of the lively flux responsible for arranging the material into its lasting form.

This book's emphasis on mise-en-scène and mise en abyme is thus meant not as a corrective to genre analysis—indeed, this book invokes genre throughout—but rather as a way of highlighting what is dynamic in the sedimentation process, and (leaping now from geology to geography) of tracking processes that oscillate between contingency and coherence. In a world of such combined and uneven developments, history seems to become increasingly convoluted as the scope expands in scale. We see this widening geopolitical gyre in *The Host*, whose monster is the result of a criminally irresponsible decision by a US military physician to dump hazardous chemicals into the Han River in Seoul. Based on an actual incident that was widely reported in the Korean press, the decision in the film turns out to have tremendous consequences that demand the attention of governments, militaries, and international health organizations. The allegory of monstrous exploitation played out in spectacular scenes of the beast rampaging through Seoul urbanscapes becomes even more complicated when we see that the monster's attempt to feed itself is juxtaposed with poor Korean orphans practicing *seo-ri*—the right of the hungry derived from Korean traditional rural practices to steal food in order to feed themselves. The monster is thus both city and country, both foreign and native, both metropole and colony. The blending of these contradictory concerns within a single figure exemplifies the kind of entanglements that Bong is so skilled at exploring.

As Donna Haraway has eloquently suggested, "the only way to find a larger vision is to be somewhere in particular" (590). The global view is always a view from somewhere specific. But as the previously described invocations of mise-en-scène and mise en abyme demonstrate, the effort to understand the relationship between somewhere in particular and a larger vision can lead to a hall of mirrors. Addressed to such confusions, Bong's emerging geopolitical point of view has much to do with South Korea's position in a transitional historical moment. Having entered the global marketplace under the wing of US dominance and as a subsidiary of Japanese postwar reconstruction, the nation developed into one of the largest economies in the world at a dizzying pace, becoming a semi-imperial power with a robust export economy and eventually its own sub-imperial supply chain networks in less-developed regions. After the IMF crisis and as the global dominance of the United States waned, South Korea began to question the ongoing health of its historical alliance, increasingly turning to regional markets, particularly in China, to continue the trajectory of growth that it had enjoyed throughout the second half of the twentieth century. Such new ventures and arrangements, however, had their own dangers, and thus the transitional period between US decline and Chinese ascension became clouded with uncertainty. More so than for any other contemporary Korean director, Bong Joon Ho's work attempts to make sense of these confusing times at varying scales. His art attempts to map the geography of the new avenues and pathways of global exchange—be they cultural, political, or economic—as they emerge and mutate.

Figure 5. Opening shot of *Memories of Murder.*

In the manner of Haraway, Bong's cinematic imagination is always grounded in a specific position (and mise-en-scène), even when the view is capacious and refractive. Making explicit this oscillating perspectival strategy, Bong Joon Ho's *Memories of Murder* begins and ends with very different views of the same place. The opening shot is of a young boy crouched in a wheat field, peering intently at grasshopper that he carefully plucks from a wheat plant (figure 5). We return to this field at the end of the film as the closing credits roll, but this time we are offered a landscape shot at greater remove, with the cloudy horizon in the background. Presumably, and in the manner of mise en abyme, there are many grasshoppers in the field and perhaps even other young boys looking at them, but they remain invisible now as our pupils widen and our attention is drawn across the waving fields of wheat and upward with the scrolling credits toward the sky. At the broadest level, the film explores the affordances of different critical methodologies in the attempt to ascertain the best way to solve a befuddling crime, but the effort fails, ultimately revealing the shortcomings of both perspectives manifested in these framing shots. The one immersive and granular, the other cool and removed: neither offers enough capacity to solve the crime, which remains unsolved in the film.

Accordingly, Bong's body of work situates its audience at various distances from its objects of scrutiny, not just literally by way of camera

manipulation but conceptually as well. Sometimes we are close; sometimes we are far. In *Barking Dogs Never Bite*, the bulk of the story
takes place at the apartment complex where Bong himself lived while
he was making the movie. In *Okja*, the story follows the global routes
of the Mirando Corporation's transnational business ventures, against a
challenge posed by the Animal Liberation Front, which seeks to throw
a wrench in operations that otherwise proceed smoothly despite their
massive scale. But whether we are talking about neighbors in small
apartment units getting on one another's nerves or multinational corporations flicking away the nuisance of ecoterrorists, the social relations on
display in these stories inevitably become snarled, a condition that only
becomes more byzantine as the scale widens. Indeed, as Bong's work
develops over his career, we can see how local frames frustrate global
dynamics and vice versa. The house in *Parasite*, with its Cold War bunker
and Western iconography (both its modernist aesthetics and its Native
American preoccupations), might serve as a mature example for how a
single figure might access multiple perspectival scales. Derived in part
from the classic Korean film *The Housemaid* (*Hanyŏ*, 1960), *Parasite*'s
house is domestic in at least two senses of the term (family home and
nation), but it is also continually infiltrated by extradomestic entities, be
they in the form of the hired help, who turn out to be wolves in sheep's
clothing, or in the form of the transnational capital that fuels the liveli-
hood of the house's proprietors.

The house turns out to be uniquely Korean not because it fends off
these external influences but precisely because it remains subject to
them. Emerging from postwar poverty, South Korea was able to rapidly
accumulate wealth through a program of authoritarian developmentalism, in which the strong dictatorial state strategically orchestrated
domestic corporations (*chaebol*) to prevent internal competition and
ramp up national competitiveness in global markets. This grand venture initially took advantage of extremely low costs in labor-intensive
industries like textiles in the context of Western deindustrialization. It
eventually moved into more capital-intensive enterprises like chemicals,
automobiles, and technology, leading to the flourishing of giant multinational conglomerates like Samsung, LG, and Hyundai, which dominated
national markets and became globally competitive. This coordinated

state strategy, which earned the dictator Park Chung-hee a surprising amount of praise and even affection despite the frequently harsh authoritarianism, was only possible because of South Korea's privileged role as a devoted US client state in the Cold War world order. Under these circumstances, the United States was happy to support this burgeoning example of Western-style capitalism flowering in Asia—the so-called Miracle on the Han—as a bulwark against the rising tide of Asian communism. Even when critics began to call attention to the discontents of compressed modernity, the power of this developmental period in postwar Korean history remained a solid ideological pillar and the object of a good deal of nostalgia.

The house in *Parasite* is a fuller realization of the dynamics we noted in the visiting rooms in the jail at the end of *Mother*. Its highly localized mise-en-scène demarcates a contained space that different parties compete for control over and thus becomes overdetermined by external influences. In *Mother*, the visiting room signified the hinge between individual interest and social responsibility. In *Parasite*, the house toggles between national and geopolitical concerns. That is, it is a contained space that nonetheless indicates and resonates with other places and histories: US–Native American wars in the nineteenth century, the Korean War, the global technology business. But as in the case of mise en abyme, the revelation of this scalar connection between the localized site and the larger structures it stands for produces claustrophobic disorientation instead of big-picture comfort; the localized conflicts are revealed to be symptomatic of systemic problems. In this manner Bong Joon Ho views the world from South Korea's semiperipheral position in the world system at the beginning of the twenty-first century, sedimented in between the rock and the hard place of declining US and ascending Chinese power. It is powerful enough to have a seat at the proverbial table of geopolitical governance but not powerful enough, militarily or economically, to pursue more autonomous courses of action. Such a semiperipheral position thus requires keen attention to shifting patterns, uncertain alliances, and emerging trends. Bong Joon Ho's cinematic sensibility arises from the exigencies of this tenuous position, in which survival depends on the ability to sense the subtle movements of the ground as it shifts beneath our feet.

Increments of Modernity: *Barking Dogs Never Bite* (2000) and *Memories of Murder* (2003)

Bong Joon Ho's first two feature films, *Barking Dogs Never Bite* and *Memories of Murder*, struggle with the troubling questions provoked by modernity through serial killer narratives, in which the task is to understand a fundamentally incomprehensible crime. Although both films focus on serial killings, the films differ in tone. *Barking Dogs Never Bite* is a dark comedy with elements of melodrama. The protagonist, Yun-ju (Lee Sung-jae), is a struggling humanities graduate student, who is by turns frenetic and melancholic as he expresses frustration regarding his thwarted ambition of obtaining a university faculty position. The film's serial killer plot turns on a series of pet dogs that disappear from an apartment building where Yun-ju lives. Instead of operating as a thriller, however, the film is more sociological in sensibility. Its setting in a densely populated building complex opens up questions about how modern life has reorganized social relations and the notion of neighborly responsibility. In contrast, while *Memories of Murder* does contain a fair amount of humor, mostly in its depictions of bumbling backwater cops, it is ultimately a more austere reflection on the Hwaseong serial murders, which occurred between 1986 and 1991 in the Korean countryside. The first case of its kind in South Korea, the murders remained unsolved until 2019, when Lee Chun-jae, already serving a life sentence for a different murder, finally confessed to the crime after the statute of limitations had expired (Kwon and Hollingsworth). Still unsolved when *Memories of Murder* was produced, the murders occasion for Bong contemplation on the irresolution of modernity writ large. Despite their tonal differences, the serial killer mysteries in the two films come to serve as stand-ins for larger historical crimes—crimes of modernity, crimes of the state—which demand new epistemological frameworks for thinking through formerly unthinkable affronts.

Accordingly, both films also foreground detective figures who struggle to fathom the brutality of the crime, which stands in stark contrast to the banal rhythms of everyday life. And though, nominally, these detectives attempt to identify the killer and perform their part in juridical processes, their stories of detection are meant to signify a more fundamental struggle to process the discontents of compressed modernity in

South Korea.[2] Given the life-and-death stakes of these social problems, the imperative toward knowledge that one usually ascribes to detective narratives—which are directed not only to learning the identity of the killer but also to understanding motive and context—requires a more fundamental inquiry into our basic understandings of the disorienting worlds depicted in each film. Before we can make sense of the crime, we first are required to make sense of the new social arrangements in which it is perpetrated. To address these very basic epistemological problems, both films attempt to solve their mysteries by ascertaining incremental knowledge where more complete pictures are lacking. In the manner of a detective accumulating clues, these films fetishize small, measurable certainties that might build toward larger explanations.

Early in *Barking Dogs Never Bite*, for example, Eun-sil (Kim Ho-jung) demands that her husband, Yun-ju, crack open a bagful of walnuts before he leaves for a work outing. Annoyed at the request from his pregnant wife, an incredulous Yun-ju complains that there must be one hundred walnuts in the bag. As if negotiating, she counters with a lower number—only fifty. Compromising still further, Eun-sil downs the rest of her beverage and tells him that instead of cracking one hundred walnuts, he must simply fill the empty glass with shelled walnuts before leaving. The scene demonstrates the couple's nontraditional power relationship in an otherwise patriarchal society, for which the glass of walnuts serves as an objective correlative. Seated at the table above Yun-ju, who is positioned on the floor, Eun-sil is tired from her day at work, having just come home, whereas Yun-ju, an unemployed humanities graduate student struggling to find a full-time position, must navigate his wife's annoyance to obtain permission to attend the gathering, where he hopes to make a good impression on someone with the power to get him a job. That Eun-sil ultimately gets to set the number of walnuts is telling.

The walnut disagreement foreshadows a later conflict for the couple about the distance of a store from their location on the street as they walk back toward their apartment after shopping. Eun-sil realizes that they have neglected to buy strawberry milk for her coddled dog. Yun-ju resents the dog and balks at Eun-sil's order to go back for the milk. Throwing a tantrum in disbelief, Yun-ju complains that the store is one hundred meters away, while Eun-sil counters that it is only fifty, repeating the exact numerical proportions of the walnut disagreement. The subtext here as well is Yun-ju's feeling of emasculation in his marriage, particularly over the fact that his wife is the family's primary breadwinner. He begins to pace off the distance to the store to verify his estimate, but Eun-sil ridicules him, saying that he might as well concede since he is heading there anyway. Realizing the shortcomings of his initial plan, Yun-ju instead pulls out a roll of toilet paper from their shopping bag, pointing out that the packaging claims that it is exactly one hundred meters long. With a crazed look in his eye, he proceeds to unroll it down the inclined road back toward the store (figure 6).

In *Barking Dogs Never Bite*, these physical approximations—fifty or a hundred walnuts or meters of toilet paper—accord not just to literal dimensions, as in the cramped spaces of the working-class apartment building depicted in the film, but also to the attempts of characters to understand the changing social arrangements of the residents that dwell within these spaces. Yun-ju wants to live a more meaningful life but feels diminished by circumstances out of his control. His childish arguments involving walnuts and toilet paper are compensatory efforts to claim agency. But as he realizes belatedly in the film, it is ultimately his wife who bears the more significant burden. After having worked for her company for eleven years, she is unceremoniously released during her pregnancy with a small retirement severance, most of which she had

Figure 6. Yun-ju unrolling a roll of toilet paper down a sloped street in *Barking Dogs Never Bite*.

planned to use to bribe the dean of Yun-ju's university for a permanent position for her husband. Her only personal indulgence is the dog, for which she has used a small portion of the severance. Yun-ju subsequently becomes overcome with guilt over how badly he had misunderstood his wife's situation while fixating on his own troubles. To make up for his selfishness, he ventures off in search of the dog, burdened with the realization that his previous inability to appreciate concerns outside of his own has prevented his awareness of the fundamental social relations that connect him to the community around him.

Walnuts and toilet paper give way to bananas in *Memories of Murder*, Bong's subsequent film, the visibility of which at international film festivals began to open for the emerging director a more global audience. Blowing off steam in a room salon, a distinctively Korean establishment where men can drink and sing karaoke in the company of hostesses, Detective Park (Song Kang-ho) launches into a diatribe about the difference between methods used by the US Federal Bureau of Investigation (FBI) and Korean investigative methods. Waving around a banana as he speaks, Park leans into Detective Seo, who serves as the film's primary advocate for scientific investigation, and asserts that the FBI needs to operate in this manner because "they got so much fucking land!" He continues, "If you don't use your brain, it's too much ground to cover." In contrast, Korean police can cover the entirety of Korean land "using just your two legs . . . because our land is the size of my dick," he says, pointing the banana at Detective Seo, who is (now uncomfortably) eating a banana of his own. The analogy is as simple as it is vulgar: banana, male sexual organ, and national geography align in Detective Park's drunken soliloquy. And though Detective Seo resists his counterpart's antiquated methods and bristles against his coarseness, he can't but help, as their homosocial relationship develops throughout the film, to ingest the truth of Park's insight.

This methodological difference in crime-solving techniques organizes the film's plot. The formal investigation in the film is staged as a competition between Seo's scientific methods and Park's more intuitive approach, with Seo's method gradually proving more effective as they proceed. Nevertheless, the kind of certainty implied by Park's banana remains a primary if elusive goal throughout the investigation, particularly as even Seo's modern methodology proves insufficient. As the team moves through a series of suspects, initially based on specious evidence, and later backed by what seems to be hard proof, certainty becomes increasingly difficult to ascertain. Although the fact that the Hwaseong serial murders were unsolved is well known to Korean audiences, the progressive movement of the investigation in the film toward understanding remains compelling. We gain confidence in the detective's efforts, though we are already aware of their failure. But when the final and most likely suspect is proved innocent in the film's climax by a DNA test, which had to be sent to the United States for processing, Detective Seo abruptly abandons his principles and reaches for a different sort of phallus, a gun, out of frustration. Park pushes his arm as Seo fires, allowing the innocent man to scamper away through a dark train tunnel. The detectives have worked with extreme diligence, even getting past their original antipathy for each other in the interest of justice, but it has been a useless effort. They are no closer to solving the case at the end than they were in the beginning. And as their protracted investigation proves futile, so too do the knowledge systems that underwrote it.

In a context so thoroughly defined by uncertainty, figures like walnuts, toilet paper, and bananas function as increments of provisional certainty that seem otherwise absent from modern Korean life after a dizzying period of rapid development. This period ended in crisis and left ordinary people to question the assumptions on which their sense of modernity was built. Figures of certain measurement in situations defined by ambiguity, the examples of incremental knowledge in these films thus imply a deep reassessment of the habits of mind that had been taken for granted for decades. On what certainties can we now depend? In this context, *Barking Dogs Never Bite* and *Memories of Murder* ask very basic questions about the worlds they articulate. How do we make sense of everyday life when it comes to seem less ordinary and more like the scene of a crime?

Yun-ju's Back

Barking Dogs Never Bite begins and ends with a shot of Yun-ju's backside, but the relationship to the diegesis is different in each case. In the film's opening shot, Yun-ju is alone in his apartment looking out the window while talking on the phone with his friend when he becomes distracted by the sound of a barking dog that seems to be coming from somewhere inside his apartment complex. The perspective here is voy-euristic, a camera observing an otherwise private moment. In contrast, though the film's final scene begins with a similar shot of Yun-ju as he looks out the window of a lecture hall before class, the perspective here is aligned with the students who fill the classroom behind him. Here, the perspective is social, reflecting the view of the students in the diegesis. Views of Yun-ju's back constitute a leitmotif in the film, ulti-mately reflecting the difference between his initially solipsistic view of the world and one that acknowledges social responsibility. Most notably, Yun-ju's back becomes important when the apartment complex's office worker, Hyun-nam (Bae Doona), chases Yun-ju through the building after witnessing him throw a dog off the roof. Their chase ends when Hyun-nam runs into a suddenly opened door, giving Yun-ju the chance to escape without revealing his identity. A violation of the apartment's policy against pets, the dog had been one in a series of yappy nuisances that had annoyed Yun-ju, whose nerves had been on edge because of his bleak job prospects. But at the end of the film, after learning that the dog he threw off the roof had been the only companion of an elderly woman, who passed away shortly after learning of her beloved pet's fate, Yun-ju is racked with guilt and confesses to Hyun-nam that it was he that she had been chasing earlier in the film. The form of his confession again highlights his backside. "Look at me from behind," he instructs, "Don't I look familiar?" Hyun-nam does not understand, so Yun-ju begins to run while she follows, reenacting their earlier chase (figure 7). Eventually, they pass a group of young women running in formation. Yun-ju pumps his arms in his distinctive way until Hyun-nam finally remembers. "Yes, it was me," he confirms.

As in the final scene in the university classroom, Yun-ju's back is here made the object of diegetic vision. The form of Yun-ju's confession, showing his backside, accords then with his broader transformation in the film, from a self-absorbed melancholic preoccupied with his dead-end career to a more empathetic resident of the apartment complex who becomes aware that his actions affect those around him, be it the elderly woman, who suffers from the loss of her pet, or his own wife, who suffers from a misogynistic work environment that refuses to ac-commodate working mothers. Yun-ju's recognition that his backside is visible thus signals the emergence of a sociological sensibility in the film

Are you crazy?
What are you doing?

Figure 7. Yun-ju and Hyun-nam reenacting their
earlier chase in *Barking Dogs Never Bite*.

from self-obsessed individualism. This transformation, his eventual and
reluctant realization of his own social immersion, in turn indexes the
social dynamic that inheres in the film's primary setting, the modern,
Korean apartment complex, which fosters isolation and atomization,
ironically, by placing people in greater density. In this manner, the film
situates the drama of Yun-ju's emotional development within the larger
historical rubric of Korean developmentalism, for which these kinds
of apartment complexes are signatures. In this respect, it is a version
of what Pamela Robertson Wojcik calls an "apartment plot," that is, a
story that is not just framed in this setting but whose narrative is driven
by it (6). Of course, the Korean apartment has different geographic
coordinates than its American counterparts in Wojcik's study.

If you drive around Seoul today, you will still periodically see large
complexes of aging mid-rise apartments, consisting of identical concrete
structures usually emblazoned with the name of the Korean conglomerate that built them. Many of these buildings have already been torn
down and replaced with the newer, taller structures that now dominate
the skyline. Seoul did not always look this vertical. It was not until the
construction of these apartment buildings, beginning in the 1960s and
accelerating in the 1970s, that apartment living became the primary
way of life for Seoul residents, as the city's population rapidly increased

and the city's borders rapidly expanded east and south from its historical core north of the Han River. In Gangnam (literally *river south* in Korean), where farmland was converted into urban space, this type of apartment complex flourished, propelled in its popularity by Koreans who flocked to this scene of modern living. This construction activity became particularly robust around the watershed year of 1988, the historical moment when the war-torn nation could announce its entrance into the world economy as a prosperous and modern democratic nation, now freed from military dictatorship.

At this important historical juncture, a new neighborhood south of the Han River at the easternmost point of urban development in Seoul arose around the sports complexes built for the 1988 Olympics, a symbolic moment in modern South Korean history that marked both the nation's entrance onto the global stage and the end of authoritarian rule. This was also the neighborhood where Bong Joon Ho's family settled after moving from the smaller city of Daegu while Bong was in elementary school. By 2000, when *Barking Dogs Never Bite* was released, such apartment complexes with their shoddy construction had already lost their initial shine, increasingly serving as vexed figures for a modernizing turn in which heady utopian urbanism had given way to disappointment. Expressions of this sort of vexed modernity are manifold in the film. Most obviously, the darkly humorous conceit of serial dog murders, a source of embarrassment for Bong later in his career, highlights the tension between a persistence of the Korean tradition of eating dogmeat stew (*poshint'ang*)—as enjoyed by the building's janitor and the indigent man who resides surreptitiously in the building—and the new modern trend toward pet ownership (see Ku 143). Anticipating the subterranean bunker in *Parasite*, the building's basement in *Barking Dogs Never Bite*, where the meals representing a bygone era of abject poverty in Korean history are generally prepared, serves then as persistent subconscious for the modern structure that sits above it.

It is also a site of haunting. When the building manager interrupts the janitor's meal early in the film, the janitor tells a ghost story about a man named Boiler Kim. From the story, we learn that the building was indeed built around 1988 and that, like many buildings of the period, it was built hastily. Boiler Kim was a genius with fixing boilers, which would require premature attention because of the substandard building practices. According to the story, after repairing the boiler in the building, Boiler Kim accused the builders of using cheap materials and embezzling the money. In the argument that ensued, Boiler Kim fell backward, hitting his head on a protruding nail and dying there on the spot. Faced with the prospect of blood on their hands, the greedy builders buried the body of Boiler Kim inside one of the building's walls, taking a solemn vow of silence. Their crime was never exposed, but the sound of Boiler Kim mimicking a spinning boiler can be heard every night as a kind of telltale heart, reminding residents above of the wrong that was done to him by the criminal builders and of the fraudulent modernity that the building represents.

Boiler Kim's symbolic function as modernity's conscience is reprised, crucially, in Hyun-nam, who also serves as a witness to a crime. An employee of the apartment complex's management office, she loses her job at the end of the film just as Yun-ju finally gains employment. She loses her job because she spends too much time outside of the office, becoming the serial killer plot's primary detective figure, a task she first takes on when she sees through a pair of binoculars Yun-ju throw the dog off the roof, in a moment that gestures toward Alfred Hitchcock's *Rear Window* (1954). Hyun-nam is not terribly disappointed by her terminated employment, however, because hers is not fulfilling work. Throughout the film, we see Hyun-nam become preoccupied with fame as an escape from the banality of daily life. She lingers too long at subway stops reading the tabloid newspapers, missing her train on one occasion. She falls for a late-night prank caller who pretends to be a television show producer trying to get in touch with her on behalf of a famous singer that supposedly named Hyun-nam as his first love. Later, her attention is piqued when she watches a television news story about a female bank employee who is awarded a commendation for fighting a bank robber. Her interest in fame, however, is less motivated by a deep desire to be a celebrity than it is by a more modest aspiration to simply feel present in modern life and to interrupt the repetition of her unremarkable daily existence.[3] In the opening of the film, we see her sleepy commute to the building's management office (she often sleeps on trains), where she arrives before the other employees to perform the menial cleaning and preparations for the workday. Hyun-nam is a walking contradiction: we see her asleep and startled when she is abruptly awakened (as happens repeatedly throughout the film), but she is also the film's primary detective figure and an attentive one at that. She throws herself into the investigation of the dog killings precisely because it offers a reprieve from her mundane life. She finally gets the opportunity for notoriety when the indigent man is caught for the dog murders, for which he is only partly responsible, but the television news segment about the incident omits the interview with her that the film crew had recorded.

Though ultimately denied recognition, Hyun-nam figures the idea of social responsibility to the otherwise solipsistic Yun-ju when he reenacts their earlier chase through the apartment complex at the end of the film. Unlike the first time, the reenactment foregrounds the view from behind and the fact that his actions have consequences for other people, despite his earlier failure to recognize this basic fact. Like Eunsil, who also loses her job in the film, Hyun-nam seems to exist in the film primarily as a foil to Yun-ju, a Boiler Kim to his reluctant (emotional) development, a figure who must recede for him to ascend. The final scene of Yun-ju beginning his lecture, appropriately on modern behaviorism, is strikingly subdued and not triumphant. His acknowledgment of the audience's perspective as he stands before his class amounts to an acknowledgment not only of the fact of social relations, a lesson that he has learned through the course of the film, but more importantly of social competition. His success, in other words, has depended on the failure of others. In fact, the job only opened in the first place because his colleague was tragically killed by a subway train after a night of drinking with the dean, as part of the same kind of bribery ritual that Yun-ju later undertakes. More proximately, Yun-ju only has the funds for the dean's bribe because of his wife's misfortune. The timing of Hyun-nam's firing from her job, just as Yun-ju successfully obtains employment, simply makes clear the film's central insight about modern living: we are not just more proximate in the sense that we live closer to one another and thus can be annoyed by the neighbor's yapping dog or his tendency to pound walnuts on the floor. More significantly, our fates become more radically intertwined to the degree that one's success must come at someone else's expense. As Boiler Kim's subterranean haunting reminds us, the apartment complex is a site not of utopian community but of hierarchy and fierce competition, a dog-eat-dog world in which neighbors quickly discover the structural antagonisms that divide communal interests.

Open Crime Scenes

If the central drama of *Barking Dogs Never Bite* negates the fantasy that inheres in both Yun-ju's self-absorption and modern apartment living, *Memories of Murder* in an early scene offers a similar proposition about crime scenes. Playing with the locked-room premise that organizes investigations in a forensically inclined strand of detective fictions, from Edgar Allan Poe's classic story "The Murders in the Rue Morgue" (1841) to the many iterations of the CBS television forensics procedural *CSI: Crime Scene Investigation* (2000–), which became very popular in South Korea in the period, *Memories of Murder* depicts the crime scene against convention: it is an open, radically permeable space, not frozen in time as the conceit usually demands. Rather than being cordoned off by police barriers and yellow tape, the open field where the second corpse is discovered is inundated with activity and thus obtains a surprisingly theatrical quality (figure 8). Spectators gather along the road bordering the field, some of them accidentally sliding down the embankment below; a tractor rumbles over a footprint, destroying a potential clue; and the presence of reporters at the scene, taking photographs of a rural police force unaccustomed to dealing with such a high-profile case, threatens an even wider, national audience than the already-large gathered crowd. The scene comprises a single long take, shot with a mobile camera, following Detective Park from the footprint on a dirt path across the field to the corpse and back to the path again, where he is too late to stop the tractor. All the while, Park's running commentary—more P. T. Barnum than Sherlock Holmes—punctuates the various elements of the chaotic scene. He yells at the bystanders, directs the hapless police officers, and angrily chases down the tractor. His efforts to maintain order, however, are ineffectual.

As in the locked-room mystery, the crime scene is understood to be a kind of text, a site of forensic inscription that awaits the intervention of the genius detective who will interpret the available clues. Western detectives in this context are thus often fashioned as intellectuals (C. Auguste Dupin, Hercule Poirot, Gil Grissom), whose work of rigorous contemplation allows them to synthesize the various clues into a narrative account of the crime, the rehearsal of which provides closure to the mystery that the discovery of the corpse opens. In this scene from

Figure 8. The chaotic opening crime scene in
Memories of Murder.

Memories of Murder, in contrast, the potential sanctity of the crime scene as a self-contained, formalist text quickly gives way to a social unruliness, in which many different interests vie to determine the meaning of the scene, as they move through cordoned-off space and trample the evidence. This room's lock is broken.

The surprising openness of the crime scene in the film reflects the open nature of the case on which the film was based. The case was open not just in the sense of being unsolved (it would finally be closed in 2019) but also in the sense of having an indeterminate historical meaning. Occurring in the late 1980s and the early 1990s, the infamous Hwaseong serial murders became part of South Korea's national mythology and were associated with the darker side of modernization, marking the end of a certain kind of premodern innocence. In addition to *Memories of Murder,* which was itself based on a theatrical play, the murders also received several different artistic treatments in other films and TV series, including *Gap-dong (Kaptongi,* 2014), *Signal (Shigŭnŏl,* 2016), and *Tunnel (T'ŏnŏl,* 2017). The fact that the murders themselves remained unsolved until 2019 not only gave them an open-ended quality but also justified their appropriation in these fictional reenactments, in which the murders served as a loose frame for creative license. *Signal,* for example, is a time-travel narrative in which a magical walkie-talkie allows a detective in 1989 to communicate with a colleague in the present. *Memories of Murder*, for its purposes, uses the murders to think about the end of the authoritarian period in 1987, and thus only depicts the investigation through that year, even though the actual murders continued until 1991.[4]

Perhaps in this context, it is not surprising that *Memories of Murder* is preoccupied with reenactment as a form of serial behavior that ultimately doubles that of violent murder. Early in their investigation, the police target a mentally disabled boy based on thin evidence, and brutally coerce him into a confession. To make the case, they stage an elaborate reenactment at the actual crime scene, complete with a younger male officer in drag posing as the victim. The whole endeavor is quickly revealed to be a farce, and the detectives are disgraced by the media for their cruelty and ineptitude. Later in the film, the detectives attempt a sting operation, a sort of pre-enactment, in which a female detective wears red clothing on a rainy evening, according to details of the previous murders, to lure the killer out into the open. It does not work. Still later, a worker in the nearby concrete factory, secretly aroused by the sexual nature of the crimes in his community, visits one of the murder sites late in the evening to masturbate, before being caught by detectives who are themselves there to perform a shamanistic ritual in a last-ditch attempt to make progress on the case. Such reenactments, highly ritualistic if ludicrously comical, not only fail to solve the murders but also, in their increasingly absurd recursion throughout the film, signal the fundamental problem: despite all this activity, the investigation never really progresses in any meaningful way. What we get instead is a series of seemingly promising leads that all turn out to be dead ends. And because these reenactments occur in the absence of real knowledge, they come to seem like serial exercises in provisional coherence—so much walnut counting.

In detective fiction, a clue is an indeterminate rhetorical figure that represents several possibilities, and a fact is a stabilized clue (Moretti 145–46). A clue that leads to unproductive investigative directions is commonly referred to as a *red herring*, so named after an old technique supposedly used to train hounds to follow animal scents during a hunt, with the pungent fish meant to distract the hound from what ought to be the actual object of its concentration. Red herrings abound in *Memories of Murder*. We move in the film from a list of highly unlikely suspects collected in Detective Park's notebook (the product of his shoddy investigation) toward increasingly plausible possibilities, until Detectives Seo and Park come to agree on their suspicion toward Park Hyeon-gyu (Park Hae-il), a factory office worker with soft hands and a college degree. But though we feel that the investigation has finally made progress, the DNA analysis that finally arrives from the FBI lab proves Hyeon-gyu's innocence, leaving the detectives frustrated and angry, tempted to ignore the science and mete out the justice they feel is deserved. Like with all the suspects we have entertained throughout the course of the film, the case against Hyeon-gyu turns out to be another distraction that takes us further away from the truth, which seems to recede with every passing murder.

But more than mere distractions to throw viewers off the scent, red herrings in the film retain their original pedagogical function as objects used to train hounds. That is, the hound was to develop a kind of comparative ability from which it could distinguish between the obvious scent of a fox and the more pronounced smell of fish. In an investigation with no shortage of theories—Detective Park at one point becomes convinced that the perpetrator has no pubic hair and so visits local bathhouses in search of a man fitting the profile—red herrings turn our attention more broadly to crime's accoutrements, the culture that surrounds it. Most importantly, we notice the police force itself, which is incompetent, arrogant, or brutal depending on where one looks. We note the various reactions as well within the community to the crimes— from abject terror to perverse titillation to outright complacency. As we move in this manner from specific clues to general characteristics, our attention turns to broader historical phenomena. The discovery of a corpse in a concrete ditch in a town whose main industry is REMICON (ready-mixed concrete) reminds us of the massive domestic construction in the late 1980s of the kind of apartment complexes that *Barking Dogs Never Bite* depicted and that Boiler Kim haunted.

Appropriately, then, the primary adjudication in the film comes at the expense of the detectives themselves, who are treated harshly in the press. In a restaurant we see a television news story about the trial of Mun Kang-je, an actual Incheon policeman charged with sexual assault in the period, before the violent Detective Cho (Kim Roi-ha) throws a bottle through the screen, leading to a drunken fight. Shortly thereafter, Cho himself becomes symbolically punished when his leg is amputated. Not only did the injury occur during the brawl he initiated in the restaurant, but the punishment is karmic justice for his penchant for kicking suspects (taking care to cover his boots to avoid damaging them) in the dark interrogation rooms highlighted in the film. Detectives in this way become accessories. Indeed, they are part of a police force that was notorious for suppressing dissent against the authoritarian government, and the film dramatizes this historical element of Korean policing. More importantly, they play a central role in a narrative apparatus that compulsively produces explanations that distract and even entertain, but that ultimately cover up the real violence at the heart of this society, that is, the violence of the state. It is this state violence that we hear in the background of the murder investigation, in the sound of the siren announcing a civil defense drill, in the television news story about police brutality, and in the brief montage that depicts a presidential visit devolving into a riot.

The other harsh fate in the film is reserved for witnesses. The closest the detectives ever come to ascertaining real knowledge about the case is not in the climactic investigation of Hyeon-gyu but in the brief return to an earlier suspect, Kwang-ho (Park No-shik), the mentally disabled boy whom Detective Park had tried to indict based on thin evidence and interrogative torture. Despondent, with their heads down on the metal desks in the police station, Detectives Park and Seo commiserate about their failed investigation. Seo turns to Park about something that had been bothering him about the investigation of Kwang-ho, asking Park whether he had coached the boy about the details of the murder. When Park adamantly denies doing this, the detectives deduce that Kwang-ho had been able to recite the details of a murder not because he was guilty of it but because he had witnessed it. Frantically, they go off in search of Kwang-ho, who flees the detectives, rightly distrustful based on their earlier mistreatment. The chase ends tragically when Kwang-ho accidentally gets hit by a passing train while the detectives desperately try to warn him of the danger. Because of Kwang-ho's disability, the complicity of the witness is a fraught issue in the film. While he is ultimately innocent of any wrongdoing, Kwang-ho is also unable to direct the detectives toward the real killer. He is both the victim of police violence and, as unwilling witness, an impediment to justice.

Figure 9. Magazine open to a picture of Lee
Soon-ja in *Memories of Murder.*

The police station scene in which the detectives get their epiphany
about Kwang-ho contains another detail that pertains to this line of thought
about the relative complicity of witnesses. As the detectives sit with their
heads resting on the desk, we see a magazine open before them. Although
it is not the object of attention, we are afforded increasingly better views
of it as the scene proceeds. Detective Seo at this point, frustrated by the
lack of hard evidence against Hyeon-gyu, declares that he doesn't need
witnesses and threatens to beat a confession out of the suspect. In the
moment just before their epiphany about Kwang-ho, we see that the
magazine page features a picture of a smiling middle-aged woman, visible
at the left edge of a shot of Park, who rests with his head down on the
desk facing Seo. Though the image appears for just a moment, we can
see immediately that it is Lee Soon-ja, the wife of the Korean dictator
Chun Doo-hwan and the First Lady of the nation (figure 9). A notorious
figure in Korean history, Chun Doo-hwan never explicitly appears in the
film, but his influence is felt everywhere within it. The closest explicit
reference to Chun is in the parade that is supposed to celebrate his visit
to the town, a parade that turns into a riot, escalated by Officer Cho and
other police beating up protestors. In 1996 (after the events of the film
but before its creation), Chun underwent a public trial and was sentenced
to death. The sentence was subsequently reduced to life in prison and,

in 1997, commuted by President Kim Young-sam. Lee Soon-ja is a far less infamous figure in Korean history, but she remains tarnished by her association to her husband. That the moment of realization in the film of Kwang-ho as a witness coincides with the invocation of Lee Soon-ja, then, makes us question the relative complicity of the witness. Is the witness an accessory, or can she remain blameless?[5]

It is no surprise that the film ends with the testimony of another seemingly innocent witness. Jumping to 2003, we learn that Detective Park has become in the intervening years a salesman and a family man. On a sales trip, he realizes that he is near the field in which he had examined the first corpse many years before. Asking the driver to pull over, Park takes a stroll over to the concrete irrigation channel where the body was discovered. A young girl interrupts his moment of reflection, telling him that she recently saw a man looking into the same irrigation ditch. When she asked this stranger why he was looking, he told her that he had done something there years ago and had come back to look. Realizing that this young girl has likely seen the murderer that he chased so many years previously, Park asks her what he looked like. The young girl responds in disappointing fashion, "Kind of plain, just ordinary."

The film asks its audience to bear close witness—much like the boy in the film's opening, who looks closely at the grasshopper. The boy's grasshopper, or at least a similar one, appears shortly afterward, perched on the first corpse found in the film. The metal ruler that we see Kwang-ho use at the video game arcade to push a button faster appears in the subsequent scene of interrogation, in the hands of Detective Park, who is leading the questioning. The adhesive bandage that Detective Seo helps put on a young schoolgirl confirms her identity later, when her body turns up as the last victim depicted in the film's serial murders. In addition, the film has us look closely at pictures, at documents, and at newspaper stories, all of which are held steady before the camera as part of a capacious archive of potential evidence. The film ultimately belies the strength of the investigative gaze—whether peering into the eyes of potential suspects (Park) or examining documents with precise care (Seo). But in so doing, it also draws suspicion onto the act of witnessing itself, wondering aloud not exactly about the guilt of the criminal but more so about the bystanders that allowed the crimes to proceed.

Come Outside

At the end of "Shaking Tokyo," Bong Joon Ho's contribution to the 2008 omnibus film *Tokyo!*, which packaged three non-Japanese directors (Michel Gondry, Leos Carax, and Bong Joon Ho) to produce Japanese-language vignettes set in Tokyo, the protagonist (Kagawa Teruyuki) implores a young woman (Aoi Yu) to "come outside." A *hikikomori*, or shut-in, the man has finally left his home after many years to search for the woman he has fallen in love with, a former pizza delivery worker who once fainted in his apartment when an earthquake happened to strike. Learning where she lives from her replacement, he discovers that she has come to share his aversion to contact with the outside world. He thus attempts to communicate to her through an open window a realization that has only very recently dawned on him about his own life: "If you don't come out now, you never will."

The general conceit of the omnibus project, bringing in non-Japanese directors to work in Japanese with a primarily Japanese cast, affords all three films a certain whimsy. Tokyo becomes something of a fantasy space in which the directors enact a series of surreal scenarios. In Bong's case, the mise-en-scène veers off from the generally realist settings of his first two films into a dreamscape of empty Tokyo streets in a city in which everyone has become a *hikikomori* and smiling robots have replaced human pizza delivery workers. But despite the aesthetic sensibility that separates "Shaking Tokyo" from *Barking Dogs Never Bite* and *Memories of Murder*, all three films explore the necessity of coming outside the safe harbor of solitary worlds that are designed to produce an ultimately false sense of security. We see this insight in Yun-ju's belated realization of his harmful role in his apartment's ecosystem and in the widening sense of criminal complicity in the detectives' investigation of the Chun Doo-hwan era. The insights are ultimately frustrated by their own limits. Yun-ju might be said to have developed class consciousness only to the extent that he, a professor standing before his students, is aware of his class and, by extension, of the way other interests might intersect or depart from his own. And the detectives, for their part, function as slightly less slapstick versions of Keystone Cops, marked by their failures rather than juridical successes. The expression of these frustrations, however, fuels the desire for the more expansive frames of critique that Bong's next pair of films develop.

Parenting Fails: *The Host* (2006) and *Mother* (2009)

If *Barking Dogs Never Bite* and *Memories of Murder* tell stories about individuals who are surprised to learn that their lives are immersed in broader and more complex social relations than first imagined, then Bong Joon Ho's next two films, *The Host* and *Mother*, foreground specifically the relationships between parents and children to explore entanglements in larger structures of affiliation. Both films invoke the ideal of a nuclear family as the standard against which the featured families fall short, and the primary shortcoming in both cases is bad parenting by a single parent. In *The Host*, the multigenerational family lacks mothers, while in *Mother*, the family, which consists solely of mother and son, lacks a father. Long ago abandoned by their partners, the remaining single parents attempt to compensate for these absences, with astonishingly horrific consequences despite best intentions (An 163). In turn, both examples of failed parenting become occasions for thinking about networks of affiliation beyond the family structure—be they focused on geopolitical relations or on questions of social responsibility. The actions of these parents thus reveal the dual character of family kinship, which serves both as the basis of a protective project that is ambivalent about the damage that self-preservation might inflict on nonfamily members and as a self-reflexive social formation that worries about the costs of familial relations. The dual character of families in these films thus becomes a primary site in which to investigate the discontents of Korea's compressed modernity that were thematized in *Barking Dogs Never Bite* and *Memories of Murder* and the entanglement of these problems within larger social and geopolitical systems (Chang, *South* 3).

In both Western and Confucian traditions, the family has always been an important moral structure, serving as a bulwark against the depredations of modern life. The family in both contexts frequently functions as the object of nostalgia, symbolizing a more wholesome past. We know however that it is also an ideological construct covering over a good deal of contradiction; the family idealization has proved useful for valorizing a range of economic arrangements while obscuring their inequities. In the postwar United States, the family wage—with its gendered division of labor into the primary breadwinner (a man), who would venture outside the house, and the domestic worker (a woman), who would manage the housework—highlighted the virtue of Fordist industrial economies while eliding the hierarchies and exclusions from the labor pool of those who could not enjoy its benefits (Black, agricultural, and domestic workers) (Cooper, *Family* 8). In post–IMF crisis Korea, the family business became a widespread alternative source of income in the context of massive unemployment and had the additional benefit for the Korean state of making a robust welfare system seem unnecessary.[6] *The Host* and *Mother* both indulge in the fantasies of family ideology and at the same time call attention to the contradictions within it. We might come to understand the family unit in this pair of films as articulating the collective interests of a group that take precedence even as they are revealed to have devastating consequences. The family's fight for survival obtains a distinctive moral character that reflects its historical privilege, but we also see just how much harm is done in the name of survival.

The moral and ideological ambiguity of the family becomes particularly manifest in *The Host* and *Mother* in the consequence of failed parenting, a primary preoccupation of these films. After the initial prologue in *The Host*, when we learn about the monster's genesis, one of the first lines we hear as the film introduces us to the central family in the film is "appa" (dad). And at the very end of *Mother*, the last line spoken by Do-joon (Won Bin) is "ŏmma" (mom), as his mother hurries off to catch her bus. Despite the use of the familiar terms of address, as opposed to *abŏji* (father) and *ŏmŏni* (mother), the circumstances of each case belie the intimate affection usually implied in the form of address. In *The Host* scene, the line is called out by a young girl passing the store where Gang-du (Song Kang-ho) is sleeping on the job, causing him to stir momentarily and incorrectly believe that it is his own daughter calling him. In the scene from *Mother*, Do-joon's address to his mother comes directly after the revelation that he is aware that she murdered a homeless man to cover up Do-joon's crime. Do-joon had just returned her acupuncture kit, which she had accidentally left at the crime scene. His mother is distraught not just by the revelation of her guilt but even more so by Do-joon's cool attitude about her crime and by implication his own.

Mom and dad in these films fail in different ways. The mother is overprotective: her horrific cover-up of her son's murderous act (by killing the only witness) becomes an extreme example of her doting. We see a less consequential but illustrative example of this overprotective drive early in the film, when she shamelessly examines Do-joon urinating against a wall while waiting for a bus and insists that Do-joon drink an herbal medicine that she holds to his face while he is still urinating. Gang-du in *The Host*, in contrast, is underprotective. He fails to rescue his daughter from the monster in its first appearance at the park by the Han River, where his family runs a small store catering to park visitors. Much to the later consternation of his siblings, he in fact grabs the hand of the wrong young girl, believing her to be his daughter, when the monster first terrorizes the riverfront area where the family's store sits. And though he attempts to redeem himself by saving Hyun-seo (Ko A-sung), he ultimately fails, and his daughter dies.

The point, however, is not narrowly moral. If the lesson of walnuts, toilet paper, and bananas in *Barking Dogs Never Bite* and *Memories of Murder* is that small things in Bong Joon Ho's imagination function as increments of larger phenomena, then bad parents in *The Host* and *Mother* represent more expansive examples of unscrupulous applications of power. As an example of what is arguably the most baldly allegorical genre (the monster movie), *The Host* is explicit about its implications. The ultimate bad father is the monstrous US empire at a historical moment when its grip on global domination begins to falter, particularly after the 2003 decision by the Bush administration to pursue an unpopular war in Iraq without the support of a global coalition (South Korea being a notable exception); the film explicitly alludes to this historical moment.[7] As we will see, the allegorical implications of the film's monster are more complicated, but its origin story—a reprehensible, real-life incident in which a US military doctor ordered the pouring of a large amount of formaldehyde directly down the drain in a US military morgue and thus into the Han River—makes US power in South Korea the allegory's most explicit referent. The film, in turn, regards the hegemonic infringements of an increasingly unstable empire as a supreme form of bad parenting, by an entity whose ability to protect its charges is called into question.

More subtly, *Mother* pivots away from the gradual trajectory established in the first three films toward expanding contextual frameworks, a trajectory that will be resumed in the films *Snowpiercer* and *Okja*, which discover in globalization the unavoidable consequence of domestic modernization. If Detectives Park and Seo awaited a verdict from the faraway FBI laboratories in the United States, then examples of US institutional authority are much more present and on the ground in *The Host*, with mobile medical labs set up directly in Seoul, on the banks of the Han River. This emergency imposition on South Korean sovereignty in turn serves as synecdoche for the robust US military presence in South Korea since the Korean War, which never officially ended.[8] In contrast to the effort in the early films to track the dramatic amplification of modernizing processes in Korea, and the interest in the later films to think globally, *Mother* represents a hinge point in the middle, turning radically inward to tell a story set in a small Korean town that remains insulated from the encroachment of Western modernity. Though the narrative is set in the contemporary present, the small-town detectives in *Mother* are more reminiscent of the country yokels that populate the police force in *Memories of Murder* than of the scientific future of the profession that Detective Seo's presence in the film anticipates. Although it seems an outlier, however, the darkest film in Bong Joon Ho's oeuvre might be regarded as a pause before a fuller global pivot meant to take a final assessment of the national orientation implied in the mother figure, one that finds fault in the protectionist inclinations of both the parent and the nation, clearing the way for more agential forms of global engagement.

A Beer for the Young Girl

Gang-du's shortcomings as a father in *The Host* are not a matter of a poor attitude about parenting or a disregard for his daughter. He is generally loving, affectionate, and caring. Rather, his failures are rooted in his inability to adequately provide for and protect his child, repeating the disappointments of his own father, who is openly remorseful through-out the film about his own inadequacies as a parent. At the beginning of the film, when Hyun-seo returns from school to the family's food stand, which doubles as their home, she complains about Gang-du's unanticipated decision to send his brother in his place for Parents' Day at school. Her uncle with a drinking problem, Nam-il (Park Hae-il), showed up smelling of alcohol. Gang-du explains that he had tried to call her to let her know of the substitution, but the old unreliable phone that Gang-du had bought her, another embarrassment, didn't work. Inside the store, Gang-du shows her the collection of coins that he has

Figure 10. Gang-du giving Hyun-seo a beer to
drink in *The Host*.

been saving so that she might have a new phone, but Hyun-seo points
out that most are hundred-won coins (worth less than ten cents each).
Then upon seeing that the broadcast of his sister's archery competition
has begun on television, Gang-du hands Hyun-seo, a middle schooler,
a beer with a straw for her to drink (figure 10). She looks at him with
some trepidation, questioning this moment of parenting—"Are you sure
you are my father?"—before taking a sip. And though she complains
that the beverage is bitter, when she is later asked by a fellow prisoner
in the monster's lair what she would most like to have from the family's
store, she answers, "a cold beer."

Hyun-seo's answer comes in a conversation with a young boy who,
along with his older brother, had also been abducted by the monster
and stored for a meal in its makeshift lair in the sewer, where they are
trapped. The boy's brother died, leaving the young boy distraught, with
only Hyun-seo to console him. To do so, she tells the young boy about her
family's modest store, which seems an abundant utopia to the orphan,
who has long struggled with food insecurity. She promises that after they
escape from the monster, the boy can eat to his heart's content all the
favorite treats that he rattles off his list. The irony of their conversation
about what they plan to eat is that they themselves represent the monster's store of food. Uncannily, the CGI monster was produced primarily
by a San Francisco–based graphics company called the Orphanage. At

the time of production, visual effects capabilities in the Korean film industry had not yet fully developed into their present-day state-of-the-art form, so Bong had to depend on this partnership with a US-based firm to accomplish the desired CGI effects—a dependency that resonates with the hegemonic relationship between South Korea and the United States depicted in the film (and reminiscent of the need to send DNA tests to the United States in *Memories of Murder*). The monster's more direct thematic connection with the orphaned boys in the film, however, and with most of the central characters in general, is the fact of hunger. Most comically, Gang-du sneaks a late-night snack when confined to the medical facility, ignoring the orders of doctors who have told him not to eat before the series of tests planned for the morning. More somberly, the family returns to the store exhausted after a long day of searching the sewers along the Han River, and we see them eat silently together in an extended shot that eventually incorporates a dreamlike fantasy of Hyun-seo joining the meal. The film in fact ends with a scene depicting a newly constituted family—with the young boy taking Hyun-seo's place—eating a typical Korean meal inside their store/home on a snowy winter evening. The camera lingers as we watch the pair eat, really eat, for an extended sequence.[9]

The boys' subplot in the film leads to this dovetailing endpoint, but their other main function in the diegesis is to introduce the concept of *seo-ri*, which, as the older boy explains to his younger brother, is the right of the poor to steal food in times of need. Derived from an agrarian tradition and associated specifically with children, *seo-ri* comes up when the older boy explains that they are not being immoral in stealing food from an abandoned store. Later, Gang-du's father explains that Gang-du used to be a smart boy when he was young, but because of his own negligence as a father, Gang-du suffered from malnourishment and was forced to partake in *seo-ri*. In taking the food they find in an abandoned store, the boys are merely exercising their moral right as hungry children. The spectacle of *seo-ri*, which occurs here not in relation to agricultural produce in a rural field, but with commercial food products in an urban environment, is a deliberate anachronism. The film's entire focus on food insecurity seems anachronistic as well, given that after a brutal period of postwar poverty, rates of hunger in South Korea have remained relatively low. Though it is certainly a persistent problem among a small population, particularly among migrant communities, food insecurity (of the sort implied by *seo-ri*) has not been a widespread problem in South Korea for a few generations. Thus, the idea of *seo-ri* with its agrarian roots and strong association with premodern impoverishment seems a bit out of place in the hypermodern context of contemporary Seoul. So, what accounts for this somewhat anachronistic preoccupation?

The Host is indeed a movie filled with hungry people and beasts, but the monster as an extreme figure of hunger in the film redirects our attention from the specific social problem to the more abstract forms of monstrous hunger.[10] At the opposite end of the spectrum from *seo-ri*, in which hunger authorizes moral exemptions, the monster's insatiable appetite shifts the focus from questions of sustenance to sustainability. Under this rubric, the various allegorical aspects of the monster converge. With its origin in a US military decision to dispose of waste irresponsibly, the monster figures the unfortunate consequences of the decades-long presence of the US military in South Korea as well as the broader idea of US global hegemony. In turn, its strangely parental characteristics—bringing the children to its sewer home and caring for them with a certain gentleness, if only to save them for a later meal—recast the client state relationship between the United States and South Korea as a form of hierarchical kinship. This relationship echoes the patronizing paternalism in the opening of the film, when the US military doctor vapidly explains to his Korean subordinate (in an attempt to allay the subordinate's justifiable concerns) that "the Han River is very broad," and that they should thus be "very broad minded" about pouring chemicals into it. The monster grows from its first sighting, when it fits inside a fisherman's cup, to the horrific beast that rampages through the crowd along the Han River. In the context of the hegemonic paternalism invoked in its origin story, the threat posed by the fully developed monster begs the question of how to sustain its monstrous growth.

Made less than a decade after the IMF crisis, the worst financial crisis in Korean history, *The Host* in this context is an example of Korean IMF Cinema (J. J. Jeon, *Vicious* 15–19). Under the influence of the US Department of the Treasury, led at the time by Lawrence Summers, former CEO of Goldman Sachs, the IMF had used the crisis as an occasion to implement a series of measures that restructured the

Korean economy according to the model that it had imposed all over the world, particularly in Latin America. These measures opened the once-protected market to Western capital, weakened labor protections, and allowed for significant foreign ownership of Korean firms, including the reckless sale of Daewoo Motors, valued at the time at $10 billion, for pennies on the dollar. Economists Robert Wade and Frank Veneroso wrote in the immediate aftermath of the IMF's actions that it may have been "the biggest peacetime transfer of assets from domestic to foreign owners in the past fifty years anywhere in the world" (20–21).

In his 2017 book *The H-Word: The Peripeteia of Hegemony*, Perry Anderson notes that the term has been used in very different ways throughout its rhetorical history, ranging from material definitions that focus on money and economic imperialism to more general forms of ideological influence. Though it certainly had important institutional and ideological consequences, the IMF restructuring of the Korean economy was a hegemonic action in the most material sense; it represented an effort by the United States to maintain the attachment of South Korea as an economic subordinate. Unlike the colonial arrangements of previous centuries, as in the case of the British Empire, which extracted tribute through direct occupation and colonial governance, the neocolonial empire of the United States was maintained through a more informal system of domination, in which nominally international organizations like the IMF ensured that the global system tilted in the United States' favor. Crucially, during the height of US economic power after World War II, when the IMF was established, the United States could provide the engine for global economic growth in a rising tide that seemed to lift all boats (Arrighi 285–90). But in its decline, which accelerated at the turn of the century, the problem became how to sustain growth, and the monstrous solution was the kind of forceful extraction that IMF actions in South Korea and many other places in the world in those years effected under the thinly veiled pretense of economic aid.

A literal figure of monstrous growth and one that was conceived in native waters, the monster in *The Host* marks the point of conflict between global and domestic interests that became suddenly apparent during the IMF crisis. In this context, the IMF bailout package in South Korea becomes an uncanny, geopolitical version of *seo-ri*, the right of a hungry empire to consume what is immediately available, conceived of in quasi-moral terms. Accordingly, we witness a series of inversions: the right falls to the parent instead of the child in a process that forestalls rather than compels basic social reproduction. The ultimate bad parent, then, is US hegemony. Most immediately, it is manifested in the film by the many techno-scientific bureaucrats that probe in Korean bodies for a fantastical disease that does not exist while ignoring their own central role in a disaster of their own making. At a slightly further remove, it is also figured in the international health bodies like the World Health Organization (WHO) that offer authoritative opinions of the crisis in highly scripted press conferences that appear as television news segments throughout the film, all of which turn out to be wrong and need to be sheepishly retracted after the damage has long been done.

Working with the US Centers for Disease Control and Prevention (CDC), the WHO in the film circumvents South Korean sovereignty, opting to deploy a biological chemical called "Agent Yellow" to combat the spread of the virus. Citing Korean failures to manage the situation as justification, the decision ignores Korean citizen advocacy groups that warn of the danger of the fictional chemical, which is a clear reference to the United States' notorious use of Agent Orange during the US war in Vietnam. In depicting a health crisis that calls for the intervention of a nominally unaffiliated international organization that thinly veils US policy decisions that in turn compromise Korean sovereignty, *The Host* rescripts the IMF crisis as a viral epidemic. In the third set piece in the film's prologue, we see a pair of underlings sprinting on a bridge toward their company's chairman as he ponders suicide on a rainy day, peering into the Han River below. This was a chillingly familiar spectacle during the IMF crisis, when broken men, having lost their jobs or fortunes, jumped off bridges to their deaths in a phenomenon that came to be known as IMF suicides (see Hsu, "Dangers"). The chairman sees something moving in the water below, presumably the monster, and for a moment is distracted from his intended task. When his employees fail to see what he sees, he reprimands them and leaps to his death. His grizzly fate—only half of his body is recovered—is revealed in a television news segment just before Gang-du and Hyun-seo change the channel to the archery competition, and the implication is that this iconic spectacle of one Korean crisis has become redeployed within the film's imaginary emergency. The casualty of the IMF crisis becomes literal food for the monster, in whose figure any compulsion toward national sovereignty is reversed to invert the guest-host relationship.

Here, the shift in title from the original Korean *Koemul*, meaning *monster*, to *The Host* for the international release, doubling the generic pivot effected in the film itself from monster movie to outbreak narrative, is revealing. In her foundational account of outbreak narratives, Priscilla Wald points out that the genre overlays over nationalist discourses an alternative kinship logic that, instead of distinguishing between familiar and foreign, separates those infected from those who are immune or have not yet become sick, maintaining a highly precarious sense of community that tends toward social breakdown and anarchy (57–58; see also Hsu, "Dangers"; Yoo 48–56). Playing on Benedict Anderson's well-known notion of an *imagined community*, which functions ultimately as a synonym for the nation, Wald's *imagined immunities* offers a figure of dissolution that erodes instead of synthesizing such coherences. Ironically, even as an unprecedented monster rages through a densely populated city, the authorities in the film become more concerned about the virus for which the monster is the presumed host. This shift also entails a reversal of Wald's dyad between invasive threat and protected community. Instead of potential incursions by intruders, the problem here is ironically the host, a reversal that makes very little sense in the context of a national pandemic but obtains a good deal of clarity in the context of hegemonic empire. In an absurd turn, the issue is not the proverbial eight-hundred-pound gorilla but the room that constrains him. This reversal in turn becomes part of a larger series of inversions in which national sovereignty must give way to hegemonic precedence.[11] Hungry children must give way to greedy parents, and the rapacious appetite of a foreign intruder obtains an uncannily moral character under the rubric of *seo-ri*. Bad parenting, it turns out, is not so much a moral failing in the world of *The Host* but rather a structural feature.

Tight Frames

After an enigmatic opening in which we see the mother dance in an open field, an uncanny sight that we only come to understand fully at film's end, *Mother* begins with a scene of her attempting to be a responsible parent, monitoring her son through the open front door of her shop (figure 11). Although her Do-joon is fully grown, she feels compelled

Figure 11. The mother's tightly framed view of her son through the front door of her shop in *Mother*.

to watch him closely because of his mental disability. So, she watches him through the open door as he plays with a dog on the sidewalk across the street, while his ne'er-do-well friend Jin-tae (Jin Goo) sits idly in a chair. Cars pass by to occasionally block her view, but she still maintains a steady eye, paying more attention to him than to the dried plants she is chopping for her herbal medicine business. She will eventually cut herself at the precise moment when Do-joon suffers harm. Shooting through her narrow view of the street with little warning, the passing cars figure the threats to her generally oblivious son. And indeed, the scene ends when Do-joon steps into the street to afford her a better view of the dog, and he is hit by a passing Mercedes-Benz, which is occupied, as we soon find out, by a group of men headed to a nearby golf course.

Tight framing constitutes a leitmotif in *Mother*. Most often, it is the mother herself who is presented in this manner, by close-up shots and by objects that seem to infringe on her personal space, particularly in investigation scenes when she is looking for someone or something. The actress playing the mother, Kim Hye-ja, is legendary for her roles in more than ninety television dramas, beginning in the 1960s, and the tight framing of her face in the film is in part an homage to the small-screen melodramas with which she is often associated. Both in the hit-and-run scene described above and in these other views of Do-joon's mother, however, tight framing implies not just a nod to Kim Hye-ja's small-screen prominence but also a blinkered perspective hampered by its unobjective proximity and narrow view. The mother is too close to her son to see him for what he is—a murderer—and too immersed in her motherly duties to be concerned with the broader moral consequences of her efforts to guarantee her guilty son's release from prison. Her perspective lack breadth. We learn throughout the course of the film that her obsession with her son is in large part compensation for the guilt she feels over a botched attempt at family suicide when he was a young boy. She had fed him poison, intending to ingest it herself afterward, but the poison proved too weak to produce the desired effect. Not coincidentally, doting on her son thereafter often takes the form of feeding him healthy food and herbal medicines, practices through which she tries to atone for her earlier offense. The scene of the mother watching her son through the open door ultimately suggests, then, the extent to which her fixation on his well-being at the expense of others manifests itself as a radical perspectival narrowing. Her narrow view, in turn, fails to account for wider—one might say global—perspectives.

The narrow views produced by *Mother*'s tight framings are also suggested by the film's small-town mise-en-scène. As in *Memories of Murder*, the town's reaction to a grizzly crime throws into relief small-town dynamics. Although the police are not the bumbling, corrupt figures of Bong's earlier murder mystery, they are out of their element, self-consciously behaving as if they were characters in the techno-scientific crime scene investigation television programs that had become popular in Korea by this point, their only point of reference for crimes of this kind. So, while they seem comfortable with the new scientific methodology—the lead detective in fact comments on how orderly the forensics team is—*Mother*'s police have a good deal in common with the provincial cops in the mold of *Memories of Murder*'s Detective Park. They are happy to pin blame on the most obvious suspect under the weight of only modest evidence, which they examine in good faith but with little perspicacity beyond common sense. And although the mother's investigation is depicted as a more thorough alternative to the too-quick adjudication of the police, we eventually learn that it is even more profoundly limited by its own biases.

Although her investigation is only possible because of her intimate knowledge of the small town and its residents, most of whom she has known for years, this familiarity does not lead to any sense of communal responsibility or duty. When confronted with an actual witness, she kills him rather than accept the fact of her son's guilt. In *Mother*, criminality thus does not involve unseen agents like the deep state in *Memories of Murder*. Truth becomes banal. The very first suspect (Do-joon himself) turns out to be guilty. He killed the young girl, Ah-jung (Moon Hee-ra), somewhat accidentally when she called him *pabo*, which means fool or moron more generally but can also be used in disparaging reference to mental disability. For this reason, it is a trigger word that incites Do-joon to violence. When Ah-jung, annoyed that he had been drunkenly following her, calls him *pabo* and throws a rock at him, he angrily lobs the rock back at her with tragic results. Subsequently, the considerable effort of investigation put into motion by the indomitable will of the mother obscures rather than clarifies the truth of what is ultimately a complicated crime.

Another feature of the small-town setting of the film is the preponderance of small businesses, many of which push at the bounds of legitimacy. The mother runs an herbal medicine shop and offers acupuncture treatments to the community, despite lacking credentials. She is treated for her cut at a small pharmacy by the pharmacist, who serves as a doctor for the occasion. Her friend runs a photo shop, which plays an important role in the investigation when the proprietor remembers that the murdered girl had been interested in printing out the pictures of her many sexual partners from her cell phone. A friend of the murdered girl had made these pictures possible by selling her a "pervert phone," which features a camera that remains silent when one takes a picture (silencing the mechanical clicking sound for phone cameras is illegal in Korea); this turns out to be one of a few products and services this friend peddles to her classmates. Even the indigent man who witnesses the murder and whom the mother kills is turned into a small businessman when the mother offers him payment for an umbrella she pulls from his cart on a rainy day.

This transaction is particularly revealing about the imaginary status of these small businesses in the film because the man only takes one of the two bills she offers (figure 12). It is a striking gesture: on the one hand, it seems to diminish the drive toward profit that motivates capitalist enterprise. He takes less than is offered, and not even the torrential downpour justifies a higher price. On the other hand, the man's decision seems also to affirm the act as an economic transaction between the

Figure 12. Indigent man taking only one of two
offered bills in *Mother.*

two parties rather than an act of charity by the mother; he opts for fair
payment rather than taking what is given. The conflicted transaction is
thus part of a larger idealization in the film of small-town economics,
which are imagined to be precapitalist exchanges and an alternative to
the world of Mercedes-Benz automobiles and manicured golf courses.
Indeed, Jin-tae knows to go to the golf course in the first place after
the hit-and-run incident involving the Benz because the only reason
someone driving such a car might pass through their town is to get there.

The conflicted attitude toward capitalist exchange is also manifested
in *Mother*'s invocation of barter. Early in the film, Do-joon fishes out
golf balls from the lake in the golf course, as if they were products of
nature rather than manufactured commodities, while he and Jin-tae
wait for the Benz drivers to arrive so that they might exact revenge.
He tells Jin-tae that he is going to give the golf ball to a girl as a present. Jin-tae quickly makes the sexual underpinnings of the comment
explicit, asking Do-joon whether he has ever slept with a woman. He
hasn't, save for his mother, whom he mentions with a devious smile.
Later, he tries to give a golf ball to the proprietor of a bar to pay his bill
and leaves another—with his name written on it—at the murder scene
for Ah-jung, the dead girl. In addition, we learn through the course of
the investigation that Ah-jung had been cruelly nicknamed "rice cake
girl" because it was widely believed among the men in the community
that, coming from an extremely poor family, she would exchange sex for
rice cakes. Both cases exemplify acts of exchange that seem on the one

hand idealized as a form of precapitalist barter but on the other hand tarnished by their association with sexual exploitation.

Both the film's interest in small businesses and the invocation of barter suggest that in addition to the narrowed perspective of the mother, who prioritizes her son's well-being over broader justice for her community, the economy of the small town is also tightly framed. Indeed, the informal elements of the transactions that we witness through the film—the mother engaging in unlicensed acupuncture, a pharmacist acting as a general practitioner, a schoolgirl illegally doctoring cell phones, and even the mother undertaking the investigation herself (which she takes on with the help of Jin-tae only after she fires the lawyer, with whom she becomes dissatisfied)—signal a desire to maintain the kind of social relations that Karl Marx describes as characteristics of the feudal economy of medieval Europe, in which "the social relations between individuals in the performance of their labour appear at all events as their own personal relations, and are not disguised as social relations between things, between the products of labour" (170). *Mother*'s small businesses seem committed to keeping the economy in which they participate modest. In so doing, they seek to hold at bay the kind of social transformations that commodity-oriented exchanges enact, in which social relations between individuals become fantastically reconceived as social relations between things. At one point, Ah-jung's friend, the one who sells the pervert phones, sends the mother into a corporate big-box store to buy her some tampons, giving us a glimpse of an alternate economic universe in which a disaffected store clerk wearing a store uniform scans the barcode and mechanically puts the box into a plastic bag, but the request turns out to be a deceitful effort to ditch the old woman, whom Ah-jung's friend has come to distrust. Reliance on providers outside the tightly knit community for goods and services entails the kind of dangers posed by imports like the Mercedes-Benz, whose driver gets away with the hit-and-run. Indeed, the hit-and-run episode ends with the mother being held financially responsible for damage that Jin-tae and Do-joon inflict on the expensive vehicle, while the car's driver gets away without reproach.

If *The Host* entertained a provisionally global perspective if only to locate South Korea as a privileged site for US governmental and military intervention, *Mother* feels like an even harder turn inward toward domestic concerns. The tight framing of the film's visual aesthetics combined with its thematic interest in small businesses produces a vision of a bounded nation that views transnational entanglements as threatening. Whereas *The Host* anticipated the transnational casting in *Snowpiercer* and *Okja*, both of which were scripted primarily in English, *Mother* centers a duo of iconic Korean actors (Kim Hye-ja and Won Bin) who are best known for their Korean (pre-streaming) television roles and who have limited international profiles, and it includes no Western actors at all.[12] As mentioned above, Kim Hye-ja is a legendary figure in the history of Korean television and is famous for her portrayals of archetypical mothers, who figure classically as arbiters of domestic nationalism. In the interview that follows this essay, Bong Joon Ho describes her as "the nation's mother." Her appearance in *Mother*, then, might be understood as a self-reflexive opportunity for Bong to think categorically about the conceptual implications of the figure in the tradition of Korean postwar melodrama, which centers gender in its interrogations of nationalism (McHugh 22). Won Bin, in contrast, is known for the *infrequency* of his roles. Famously selective of his projects and reclusive by nature, he managed for a decade to maintain star status in Korean popular culture through his good looks and a relatively small number of big successes, though his infrequent employment was sometimes a source of consternation for fans.[13] We should note here as well that Bong, who has worked with his principal actors in multiple films, had not worked with either Kim Hye-ja or Won Bin before and has not again since (at the time of writing).

For all these reasons, *Mother* stands out as somewhat of an anomaly in Bong's body of work. Bong's work generally is not centrally obsessed with the idea of traumatic memory, though it is a common trope in Korean cinema and a primary concern for Korean New Wave directors (see C. Choi). Thematically speaking, the film seems more tortured and less comedic that his others, following more in the manner, both thematically and stylistically, of Bong's contemporary Park Chan-wook, specifically echoing the slightly older director's signature preoccupation with memory and forgetting. Most fully realized in *Oldboy* (*Oldŭboi*, 2003), the contrary pull toward memory and forgetting in Park Chan-wook's work encompasses the tragedy of Korea's traumatic modern history, defined by the horrors of war, forced familial and national separation, and the recursion of colonial occupation by Japan in the neocolonial arrangements of the United States. In a similar manner, Do-joon works through his hazy memories toward the fact of his own guilt against his mother's desire to use acupuncture so that he might forget his painful memories, a desire that reminds viewers of Dae-su's (Choi Min-sik) enlistment of a hypnotist at the end of *Oldboy* to help him forget that his lover and daughter are the same person. In both cases, the weight of a traumatic past yields to the easy solution of amnesia, which only ameliorates and does not obviate a stubbornly persistent pain.

There is a scene toward the beginning of *Mother* at the golf course, where Do-joon has to remind himself of his purpose, that he is there for revenge, which the peaceful setting has made him forget. This reminder seems self-reflexive, pertinent as well for the film's director working in unaccustomed terrain, as if the film needed to remind itself of the genre it was entering. In the interview that follows this essay, Bong reveals that the shooting of this scene was the first time he had ever been to a golf course. Before their antagonists eventually arrive on a golf cart and the conflict begins, there is an idyllic stretch of time during which Do-joon and Jin-tae walk through the perfectly manicured grounds and try to make sense of the space they find themselves occupying. Just as Do-joon finds himself in an unfamiliar environment, wading into the waters of a golf course lake to fish out golf balls, Bong seems in this moment to acknowledge the extent to which the concerns of the film pull him to some degree away from the directions established in his filmmaking heretofore.

The anomalous quality of *Mother*, however, becomes useful for understanding the pivot Bong makes in his subsequent films, a pivot, we might say, that culminated with the historic triumph of *Parasite* at the 2019 Cannes Film Festival and the 2020 Academy Awards. *Parasite*, along with *Snowpiercer* and *Okja*, as we will discuss later, adopts a more global perspective, even as they center Korea within that broader frame. The tight framing of *Mother*, in this context, might be regarded as a final effort to exhaust the narrow view. By looking radically inward, the film wonders about the crushing legacy of Korean modern history, feeling this legacy viscerally as a kind of radical confinement. Because any thorough investigation yields self-incrimination and the horrific realization of widespread complicity with the crimes of modernity, the remedy for this impossible claustrophobia, expressed by so many tight frames, becomes a desire to escape.

The thematically anomalous quality of *Mother* is also reflected in the film's editing, which again seems indebted to Park Chan-wook. Specifically, we see this homage in its frequent use of wipe cuts and the liberties it takes with the diegesis, techniques that are hallmarks of Park's film aesthetics in *Oldboy* and furthermore are generally uncharacteristic of Bong Joon Ho's filmmaking. *Oldboy* uses wipe cuts to produce coherence out of discontinuity. When in the film's climax Woo-jin (Yoo Ji-tae) finally reveals to Dae-su how and why he has manipulated his listener's life, the film cuts back and forth between the present scene in Woo-jin's penthouse and flashbacks using a number of wipe cuts, sometimes in conjunction with split screen effects, in order to demonstrate how seemingly disjunctive events were actually part of a highly orchestrated plot to exact revenge on Dae-su. Simply put, wipe cuts place what seemed like unconnected images and events literally next to one another. In perhaps the flashiest example, Woo-jin, who is getting dressed throughout the dialogue, opens a dresser drawer that contain his cuff links; the drawer as it opens from left to right across the screen covers over the previous shot of an unconscious Dae-su in a car with Mido (Kang Hye-jung), suggesting that Woo-jin's sharp dressing is an expression of a broader obsessive disposition that regards other people as mere accoutrements to his will. Similarly, at the end of the movie, when the hypnotist returns Dae-su to Woo-jin's apartment in the procedure that helps him forget, the camera tracks to the right while a wipe cut proceeds from right to left across the screen, using a concrete pillar in Woo-jin's fancy penthouse as a diegetic object to mark the boundary of the cut. In both cases wipe cuts are used to subordinate disparate scenes to the will of the narrator's coherence, first in Woo-jin's story about his highly orchestrated plot and second in the hypnotist's suggestive ability to take control of Dae-su's imagination, such that he believes he is not sitting in a snowy forest but has returned to Woo-jin's penthouse. In both cases the wipe cut produces a sense of spatial continuity that attempts to overcome temporal dislocation, suggesting a physical adjacency that reflects the narrator's counterfactual forced juxtaposition.

In *Mother*, similar wipe cuts are used to emphasize the act of memory, most explicitly when we see Do-joon call out at night to his mother from the prison. In the most complexly edited scene of the film, we see Do-joon's imaginative revisiting of the night of the murder. We see a close-up of his face, still bruised from a prison-yard brawl; he seems to track a sideways movement with his eyes, a movement that then gets doubled by a wipe cut that moves from left to right from behind Ah-jung in the alley to inside the house where Do-joon remembers a witness peering through a narrow opening. There are other stylized editing tricks in the sequence. At one point, the shot of Ah-jung walking from behind the tracks rewinds, and she momentarily walks backward. Furthermore, the whole sequence depicting Do-joon's memory is intercut with the mother running frantically to Ah-jung's grandmother's house. The effect is disorienting. Past and present, along with the experiences of different characters, are presented together as if part of the same continuum. The wipe cut thus functions here as part of a larger vocabulary in which memory and investigation are represented as acts of literal juxtaposition.

The other stylized feature that *Mother* borrows from *Oldboy* is atemporal juxtaposition, in which elements or characters from one part of the plot are placed anachronistically in the same scene with elements or characters from another. In *Oldboy*, Woo-jin remembers the moment of his sister's suicide viscerally in the elevator after his final encounter with Dae-su. We see him reaching downward, grasping an extended hand that turns out to belong to his long-ago deceased sister, a fact that is confirmed by the next cut, to a flashback memory of that fated scene. The counterfactual presence of his sister's arm in the elevator expresses Woo-jin's sadness. She remains literally present in the diegesis despite her death, and the memory is so affecting that Woo-jin himself commits suicide. *Mother* deploys this same trope when, for example, one of the boys with whom Ah-jung had an affair before her death remembers Ah-jung saying something about trading her phone for *makkŏlli*, a Korean rice wine favored by her grandmother. The boy looks down at his lap, where we see Ah-jung make the comment as she lies facing upward, looking at her phone. More subtly, when the proprietor of the photo store, a friend of the mother's, remember Ah-jung coming into her establishment, we see a flash of light on the right side of the screen, lighting up the darkened room where she is working at night on fixing an old photograph of Do-joon. The shot then cuts to a memory of Ah-jung and her friend entering the store on a bright day, revealing the source of the light that had appeared counterfactually in the previous shot.

In *Mother*, these counterfactual moments function in a similar manner as the wipe cut, producing a sense of continuity across a temporal disjuncture. The dead reappear in memories, which are manifested as the physical presence of their bodies, not as ghosts, but as if they were alive. But rather than offering a sense of embeddedness within a coherent social fabric, such juxtapositions parse the already tight spaces characteristic of the film's mise-en-scène into even smaller increments in the manner of mise en abyme that become disconcerting rather than reassuring. Accordingly, the uncanny scene of the mother dancing in the open field that begins the film and to which it later returns, we learn, is quite the opposite of a picture of freedom. The mother imagines herself here not alone in an open field but in the aisle of a crowded bus where she will eventually have to dance in the company of fellow travelers, a performance of innocence intended to conceal the truth of her guilt. The film is left with a difficult problem: the acknowledgment of one's embeddedness within a social body requires an acknowledgment that one's self-interest is often harmful to that same social body. But on the other hand, the fantasy of protectionism, the fantasy that one can hold at bay external forces—be they bad influences on one's impressionable son or transnational infringements on domestic sovereignty—becomes unsustainable.

Bad Protection

By foregrounding figures of failed parenting, *The Host* and *Mother* explore aspects of a world in which globalization seems inevitable. *The Host* worries about the problem of sovereignty when monstrous hegemonic appetites take precedence over local communal needs. The right of the hungry to access sustenance in a premodern agricultural context gives way to the right of a neo-imperial power to appropriate what it needs to sustain primacy, even if that appropriation requires conjuring fictional threats to justify it. But if a logical conclusion for this lack of sovereignty is to yearn for more protective arrangements, *Mother* undermines the desirability of this alternative by demonstrating its profound limits. Despite its inward turn toward domestic nationalism, *Mother* remains deeply uncomfortable with the protectionism (as figured by the protective mother) that such a turn entails. Most obviously, justice becomes a secondary priority to individual well-being as the social fabric of the town unravels. In this way, *Mother* makes a provisional if tentative case for globalization by foregrounding the horrific entailments of its opposite, ultimately amplifying the urgency of the need to *come outside* expressed in "Shaking Tokyo," *Barking Dogs Never Bite*, and *Memories of Murder*. An overly protected, closed-off community becomes self-devouring and full of violent threats that are not adequately scrutinized by its characteristically narrow perspectives.

The impasse between these two positions, longing for autonomy but remaining clear eyed about the abuses of parochial environments, paves the way for Bong's subsequent films, which foreground the desire to escape such strictures. In these subsequent films, the perspective widens to include transnational casts of characters and settings. Accordingly, the production and distribution of the films themselves become more transnational as well, with Bong partnering with large US-based media corporations to tell different kinds of stories.[14] Both within their dieges and without them, *Snowpiercer* and *Okja* are situated at quite a remove from the claustrophobia that frequently characterized Bong's first four films. But if these films are more cosmopolitan in sensibility as part of an effort to broaden the provincial horizons expressed in the previous films, they are also disappointed that this new orientation yields not the ideals of universal humanism in a virtuous global community but rather a vicious and expansive network of zero-sum competition. Although globalization seems to offer an external alternative to insular national-ism, it also clears the deck for more unrestrained forms of competition and struggle, free now of the fortifications designed to protect local interests against powerful intruders. Open borders and liberal markets may sound like great ideas—but not when we realize that standards for success are so demanding that mere survival becomes threatened. The desire to escape the constraints detailed in these earlier films thus proves to be more difficult to realize than first imagined, and thus the subsequent films contrive their own fantasies of escape. In this context, *Snowpiercer* and *Okja* conceive ways of escaping structures and environ-ments so expansive that they seem not to have an outside.

Fantasies of Escape (Outside):
Snowpiercer (2013) and *Okja* (2017)

In contrast to *Mother*'s intense claustrophobia and austere aesthetics, Bong's next two films embrace cosmopolitan sensibilities and Hollywood-style spectacle. They turn away from *Mother*'s vexed protectionism to engage a new fixation on competition, staged within wider transnational frameworks. The parents of the protagonists are not flawed as they were in *The Host* and *Mother* but long dead and entirely absent. The pivot in Bong's filmmaking following *Mother* is thus pronounced. A long way from the tightly framed, small-town mise-en-scène of *Mother*, *Snowpiercer* and *Okja* are more explicitly global in orientation, marking a point in Bong's career at which broader distribution networks and wider audiences became available. Although his work had reached international audiences before, initially through film festivals and then through modest distribution arrangements, *Snowpiercer* and *Okja* were conceived of as transnational productions from the outset. Both films are primarily English-language films cast with Western actors, produced with transnational crews, and distributed through major American media companies. Based on the French graphic novel *Le Transperceneige* (1982) by Jean-Marc Rochette, *Snowpiercer* was shot primarily in the Czech Republic at the Barrandov Studios. After production, the Weinstein Company (formerly Miramax) acquired the North American distribution rights. The release was significantly delayed because Weinstein in characteristic fashion demanded significant cuts from the original version, changes that Bong resisted (Vineyard). Cowritten with British journalist Jon Ronson, *Okja* was financed and produced in conjunction with American actor Brad Pitt's Plan B Entertainment. With Netflix controlling the global distribution, *Okja* is notable as the first film directed by a Korean that was released primarily on an online streaming service (D. H. Lee 155–56). As such, the film's initial release—simultaneously online and in theaters—was met with a good deal of controversy, a controversy befitting a film about a CEO's attempt to overturn her family's traditional business with new media strategies. CGV, Korea's largest movie theater chain, refused to screen the film, and rules were changed for the Palme d'Or Prize at the Cannes Film Festival, requiring films that wished to participate in the competition to have a theatrical release (Doo).

Setting the stage for the massive success of Bong's subsequent film, *Parasite*, the transnational production and distribution of *Snowpiercer* and *Okja* were accompanied by a more global mode of storytelling, in which characters are portrayed in conflict with larger systems of determination. *Snowpiercer* depicts a highly stratified dystopian world, in which individuals struggle for limited resources on a train that races across the frozen landscape on tracks encompassing the entire planet. *Okja* narrates a multivalent dispute for the eponymous "super pig" by contestants that value her for wildly different reasons, ranging from a corporate desire for profit to a young girl's personal affection to antihegemonic political resistance by an ecoterrorist organization. In different modes then, *Snowpiercer* and *Okja* express a similar wish to avoid the myopic frames that characterize *Mother*, but if this pivot toward global horizons affords a more capacious perspective, it invariably leads to new problems, which in turn engender a different set of escape fantasies. If the earlier task was to break free of narrow parochialisms, then the new objective is to escape totalizing systems for which there seems to be no alternative.

The comforts of the familiar thus give way to a more daunting arena, in which the trade-off for the wider frame of reference is unnervingly intense struggle. Accordingly, both films thematize forms of competition and are preoccupied with logistical problems stemming from the challenges of sustaining prosperity, advantage, and even life itself under difficult circumstances. We learn throughout the course of *Snowpiercer* that the train is a tenuous ecosystem and that the charge of its leader is to guard its delicate balance at all costs. While some measures limiting the consumption of rarer resources seem relatively innocuous, such sensible precautions serve as cover for the more brutal measures that must be taken to maintain population levels and the needs of the privileged classes. Instead of staging a familiar binary David-and-Goliath antagonism, *Okja* triangulates competition, adding a layer of mediation between Mija and the Mirando Corporation in the form of the Animal Liberation Front (ALF), which has its own third-party agenda in the struggle between the young girl and the massive multinational corporation. This tweak transforms what might have been a simpler good-versus-evil drama into a more complex story in which a young girl's guileless love for her pet is inserted into the intricate frameworks of global corporate capitalism and ecological activism.

Crucially, we should note that the conflicts in these films most often revolve around the large-scale production and distribution of food. Scaling up what was in *The Host* and *Mother* an interest in parents' ability to feed their children, the concern in *Snowpiercer* and *Okja* is with food infrastructures for entire societies. *Okja* explicitly revolves around the machinations of a global food corporation and particularly its investments in genetically engineered animal products. Similarly, *Snowpiercer* is obsessed with food production and consumption on the train. In the middle section of the film, which occurs in the middle section of the train, we witness several scenes that highlight the train's food production operations, from the making of the tail section's gelatinous bars out of crushed cockroaches to the agricultural endeavors established for the benefit of the train's more moneyed passengers. We also learn of the tail section's history of cannibalism, which prompted the production of the protein bars that sustain the tail section at minimal cost, as Curtis and Edgar (Jamie Bell) fantasize about the steak enjoyed by the train's more privileged passengers. So, on the one hand, these films are preoccupied with questions of social reproduction and survival in their interest in sustenance and victual consumption, but, on the other hand, the focus on corporate logistics in these films threatens to subordinate these basic needs to seemingly more big-minded concerns of ecological sustainability and fiscal profitability. Logistical complications thus become a matter of life and death.

In what becomes a sign of the logistical complexity of such operations, the notion of translation emerges as a key site of negotiation. When in *Snowpiercer* Curtis enlists the help of former security specialist Namgoong Minsoo (Song Kang-ho), who only speaks Korean, he must rely on a mechanical translator to facilitate their interactions, a role that is sometimes also filled by Minsoo's bilingual (and clairvoyant) daughter, Yona (Ko A-sung). These translation devices also serve an instrumental purpose, creatively rendering extradiegetic subtitles mostly unnecessary—except in rare cases when the Korean-speaking characters converse with one another in the film. These are imaginative attempts to surmount what Bong would later call, in his acceptance speech for Best Picture at the 2020 Academy Awards, the "one-inch-tall barrier of subtitles."[15] More significantly for the present context, they serve as figures of logistical difficulty, no doubt doubling the challenges of the translingual creative production that was *Snowpiercer*.

But beyond figuring production challenges, the emphasis on translation in these films functions as a broader rubric that foregrounds the site of potential misunderstanding and discord that emerges when logistics become especially byzantine, particularly in transnational networks of circulation. Accordingly, violence often erupts in relation to the problem of translation in these films. In *Okja*, the otherwise pacifist leader of the ALF, Jay (Paul Dano), ruthlessly beats his comrade and translator K (Steven Yeun) when he learns that K deliberately mistranslated his request to Mija for permission to proceed with the organization's plans to use Okja as a plant to expose the misdeeds of the Mirando Corporation. In *Snowpiercer*, Curtis becomes frustrated and even comes to blows with Namgoong, whom he mistakes as a drug addict preoccupied with Kronole, the narcotic of choice on the train. In both cases, the explosion of physical violence resulting from poor or incomplete translation indicates the high stakes of logistical failure in complicated systems, whether we are speaking of the work of sustaining the earth's surviving population or a multinational corporation with a complex array of overlapping business ventures—or, indeed, a transnational movie production.

If anxiety over functional translation indexes the foundational problem of logistical entropy that plagues the unstable worlds depicted in each film, then the potential salve that these films place under consideration is the notion of formalized management, a notion that both films explore through stories about *leadership*. The figure of the troubled leader in these films thus replaces the figure of the failed parent in Bong's earlier work. As the designer and principal operator of the train in *Snowpiercer*, Wilford obtains the status of deity, a status that we see indoctrinated from an early age in the school car scene, in which young children learn of his story as if it were scripture. Curtis emerges as a potentially revolutionary leader, though he initially defers to the selfless Gilliam (John Hurt), whom Curtis regards as better suited for the role. When Gilliam dies, and at the urging of other members of his insurrection, Curtis takes on the leadership mantle, only to discover its horrifying entailments at the climax of the film. In *Okja*, leadership is hotly contested. At the Mirando Corporation, the brutal Nancy

Mirando waits in the wings for her sister, Lucy, to fall on her face as CEO (with both women played by Tilda Swinton). Nancy is surreptitiously apprised of Lucy's actions by her aide, Frank Dawson (Giancarlo Esposito), a corporate double agent. In turn, Mirando is opposed by the ALF and its leader, Jay, who models with absurd aplomb the organization's paradoxical ethos, which combines revolutionary antagonism with tree-hugging pacifism. Significantly, then, the discourse of leadership in both films links revolutionary energy and corporate greed as part of the same continuum rather than as diametrically opposed. Curtis's emergence as a revolutionary leader makes him the ideal choice to take over for Wilford in *Snowpiercer*; and in *Okja*, Lucy and Jay are presented in parallel terms, both as caricatures of blinkered figureheads who insulate themselves from knowledge of their own shortcomings.

But if in *Snowpiercer* the failure of leadership is tragedy, in *Okja* it is farce. Moving away from the claustrophobic protectionism of *Mother*, the pair of subsequent films and the Hollywood dalliance they imply (in the turn from tortured irony toward over-the-top absurdism) suggest an odd linkage between globalization as a social formation and parody as an aesthetic form. Ultimately skewered through such parodic embodiments, the failure of leadership ideals in both films reveals the absurdity of managerial agency. The best-laid plans indeed go to waste, though not because they are poorly executed but because the challenges that they are meant to surmount are fundamentally insurmountable. These are problems that by their very nature can't be managed, and a large part of the exercise in these films is to demonstrate the folly of any attempt to do so. If translation indexes the site of potential disconnect, entropy, and breakdown, leadership is at best hubristic and at worst preposterous. Under such conditions, revolutionary possibility emerges only to become subsumed under more generalized forms of competition, as the fact of individual survival takes precedence over collective organization. And it is under this rubric of survival that both films entertain fantasies of escaping the totalizing systems they describe.

Sushi at the End of the World

After the unexpected victory of Curtis's band of rebels as the train passes Yekaterina Bridge, which marks the passage of the New Year on the train, and after they take Minister Mason (Tilda Swinton) hostage, we are given an education in the operation of the train's food production. We pass through an arboretum and farming car with fruit trees and planted vegetables, and then through an aquarium car populated with numerous species of fish and other ocean-dwelling creatures. Here they pause for a meal at a Japanese-style sushi bar, prepared (in a cosmopolitan twist) by a Black man in African garb. After their meal, they will pass through a butcher car where beef and poultry hang on racks. The meal presents an opportunity for Minister Mason to explain the guiding principles of resource management aboard the train. Sushi is only served twice a year, she tells them, because of the primary criterion for all consumption on the train. Like the train, the aquarium "is a closed ecological system," which means that "the number of individual units must be closely, precisely controlled to maintain the proper sustainable balance."

As the group eats their sushi—and while, at Curtis's order, Minister Mason chews on a gelatinous protein bar from the tail section—we see emerging in the landscape outside the train the snowy outline of a capsized cargo ship and next to it a shipping crane (figure 13). Displaying the detritus of a bygone world in which aspirations toward sustainability were catastrophically unrealized, this is a didactic moment, and the juxtaposition of infrastructural ruin with the group's sushi meal is not coincidental. Although distributed primarily via airplanes rather than cargo vessels, the fresh fish required to satisfy the global appetite for

Figure 13. Capsized cargo ship coming into view
as the train passes in *Snowpiercer*.

sushi in the twenty-first century developed an enormous carbon foot-print, often requiring multiple long-haul flights to get from fisherman to table in time to preserve the freshness expected by consumers (Orlov). The sushi bar on this train, although not modeled after the restaurants (popular beginning in the 1970s) in which sushi boats move on conveyor belts (known as sushi trains in some locations) (see Magnier), neverthe-less indexes a principal value of that arrangement, namely, efficiency in distribution. Wilford's sustainable sushi becomes a rejoinder to the failed ecological stewardship implied by the mass distribution of sushi in pre-apocalyptic times.

We learn that this principle applies not only to fish but to all resources on the train, including human resources. Wilford at the film's climax echoes Mason's explication and discloses the more extreme entailments of the imperative: "And this train is a closed ecosystem. We must always strive for balance. Air, water, food supply. The population must always be kept in balance." He goes on to say that optimal balance at times of overpopulation requires more radical measures: "We don't have time for true natural selection. We would all be hideously overcrowded and starved waiting for that. The next best solution is that individual units kill off other individual units." Indeed, "the great Curtis Revolution" falls under this rubric, proving to be not insurrectionary at all, but part of a grand plan to return the train's ecosystem to equilibrium. Building on Minister Mason's earlier explanation of the sustainability principle, Wilford explains to Curtis in the engine room over a steak dinner that the principle requires violent measures, implicitly associating ecologically responsible environmentalism with harsh managerial systems in which the efficiency imperative becomes tantamount to murder. Furthermore in a instance of mise en abyme, Wilford is fashioned after a motion picture executive, with his talk of Curtis's exploits as "a blockbuster production with a devilishly unpredictable plot." In this respect, Ed Harris's performance as Wilford is something of a reprisal of his role in *The Truman Show* (1998), in which Harris plays a powerful television producer who controls all aspects of the eponymous hit show. Indeed, Wilford's corporate insignia is coincidentally reminiscent of that of the Weinstein Company, which was headed by Harvey Weinstein after he changed the production company's name from Miramax and before he fell to scandalous disgrace in 2018.

The pairing of a specifically corporate form of management with ecological stewardship in the film, then, becomes volatile. It requires, for example, a robust group of middle managers to execute the harsh measures (including actual executions) required for ecological balance. In addition to Minister Mason, the train features Franco the Elder (Vlad Ivanov) as the leader of the security group that attempts to kill Curtis and his group as they move closer to the front of the train. A host of characters work in a similar capacity, including Fuyu (Steve Park), Franco the Younger (Adnan Hasković), and even Namgoong Minsoo, who was originally the train's security expert. Importantly, while there are a range of functions for these staff positions—from military to education to food distribution—all are apparently trained killers. Even the pregnant elementary school teacher (Alison Pill) skillfully wields a machine gun and kills several insurrectionists, before being killed herself.

The fact that even early education includes assassination under its job description returns us to the primary allegorical linkage in the film between management and violence. The brutal middle managers who appear in the film in serial fashion imply a disconcerting parallel between population and corporate management, a parallel that is confirmed by Wilford, who explains the workings of the train to Curtis in the engine room, before offering him the opportunity to replace Wilford as the train's primary executive. At the end of the school car scene, a character named in the film's final credits as Egg-Head (Tómas Lemarquis), a name that reflects both his job description and his bald head, distributes the "New Year eggs" (hard-boiled eggs) from a wheelbarrow as he moves through the train. He hands the teacher a basket of eggs for the schoolchildren, at the bottom of which is a machine gun. He moves past Curtis's group toward the rear of the train, and in a moment that seems to have been coordinated, he and the teacher open fire at the same time, killing several tail section passengers. The metaphorical juxtaposition is blunt: though a symbol of new life, eggs ironically become an occasion for expedient massacre. This is the moment at which Gilliam is executed by Franco the Elder, an execution that is broadcast on a television screen in the schoolroom for Curtis to witness. Immediately following this horrific scene, Tanya (Octavia Spencer) slaps Curtis to snap him out of his shock and tells him, "You have to lead us." The scene cuts back to the screen, where we see Gilliam's corpse.

Although hesitant to take leadership responsibility through the first half of the film, Curtis does so in this moment, a transformation that is punctuated by violence. But if this is the moment Curtis takes on the onus of leading the band of rebels on behalf of the oppressed class in the tail section, it also marks the beginning of another transformation in the film, from revolutionary to corporate leadership, in which the problem of sustainability becomes indistinguishable from the problem of population management. The ecology of the world of the train is bound by the fundamental impossibility of growth; no new production can occur because resources are as finite as the space itself, limited to the span of the train. So, despite the train's many wonders, its future is structurally that of secular stagnation. For those at the front of the train to be able to flourish and enjoy creature comforts, others in the tail must suffer, even as they are kept alive as a reserve army of surplus labor to be plucked as the need arises for, say, a violin player or a small child to work inside the engine.

These ineluctable dynamics determine the nature of leadership on the train. Appropriately, Curtis's first executive action is an execution: he picks up a gun from the floor and wordlessly shoots Mason in the head over her final pleas as she kneels before him. The executive must execute in the most brutal sense of the term; and one can draw a straight line from Wilford, the train's executive, to Franco the Elder, who is reminiscent of the cold assassins of modern spy fiction, to the atavistic masked executioners who confront Curtis's group at the Yekaterina Bridge battle. Dressed in dark hooded masks and wielding axes, hammers, and other crude instruments, this austere army harks back to the figure of the medieval executioner, whose mere visage was meant to strike fear and discourage dissent. Indeed, the leader of this vicious legion uses his axe to draw blood from a large fish before the battle to intimidate Curtis and his crew, a gratuitous display that explicitly violates the principles governing the consumption of fish expressed by Minister Mason.

The point here is not that absolute power corrupts absolutely. Rather, establishing an idea that Bong carries into *Parasite*, *Snowpiercer* presents an environment defined by zero-sum competition, from which cruelty must emanate as a necessary consequence. The mise-en-scène of the train implies hierarchy: Curtis and his friends have been relegated to the tail section, while others seem to enjoy more choice placements.

This placement principle not only maintains social order on the train but also structures the narrative of the film itself. The brutality of individual actors is merely an expression of the fundamentally brutal structure of the environment, which is defined by finite spaces in which growth is not possible (a train or, in *Parasite*, a single house). The discourse of ecological sustainability in *Snowpiercer* reflects the centrality of this logic, and leadership in the film is determined by this fundamental fact. So, it is not so much the failure of revolutionary ideals that Curtis confronts at the end of the film but rather the fact that such ideals are anathema to the foundational principles aboard the train, which everyone, even the rebels, cannot help but replicate. These principles exist precisely to occlude the fundamental incoherence that suffuses the train's ideology. We see in the schoolroom scene a hagiographic video about Wilford and the train that sketches out for the audience how the train works. We learn that Wilford Industries, before the disastrous end to human civilization, had managed to connect the railways of the entire world into one circular system that the train would circumnavigate over the course of precisely one year, making the route map that we see on the screen a calendar as well (figure 14).

Centering Korea geographically even though several of the emphasized dates are US holidays, the map also visualizes a major aporia in the train ideology, an aporia that lays bare the limits of the train world: the

Figure 14. Route map of the train in *Snowpiercer*.

real miracle of the train is not the engine, which has become the object of religious devotion, but the tracks. It is unexplained how a second-rate billionaire, derided by his contemporaries, managed to negotiate with all the required nations to build this system and to construct long expanses of rail lines that would cross large expanses of (nonstate) waters. And though much talk is made of engine maintenance in the film, the far more fraught question of track maintenance (in a world in which human beings cannot go outside) remains unexplored. Furthermore, we see that while the train circumnavigates its track system, the track system does not circumnavigate the planet, creating an odd disjunction between planetary and train temporality, which are coincidental (a lap around the tracks precisely takes a year) but not identical (the route of the train reverses direction rather than synchronizing with the turning earth). Indeed, the map makes the earth appear to be flat. Finally, we can extrapolate from the map and the geographic details mentioned in the film like the Yekaterina Bridge (located in Russia) that the events depicted in the film likely occur in the winter months in eastern Russia, in which such weather conditions existed even before the apocalyptic events that destroyed human life on earth. One wonders what this narrative might look like when the train dips in the summer months below the equator into South America or, later in the year, into Africa. All these details, however, are of course swept aside, and we are left with Wilford's mandate and fanatical devotion to the engine as the source of life.

The only alternative to Wilford's vision of ecological balance is Namgoong Minsoo's aspiration to get off the train, but it comes with a problem of interlinguistic comprehension. With the introduction of Minsoo toward the beginning of the film, translation becomes a matter of necessity, an extension of the logistical complications involved in advancing through the train and past the various security barriers designed to make such progress impossible. The logistical imperative leads to a negotiation in which Curtis enlists the help of the former security engineer, who designed these aspects of the train, in exchange for Kronole, mistakenly thinking that Minsoo is an addict. This practical exchange casts Minsoo and his daughter as merely expedient companions to Curtis's impassioned crew, serving an instrumental function without being swept up into the revolutionary fervor. Translation in turn is a further extension of expedience. The handheld device is barely audible when it is used and often is not used at all; it fails altogether when Minsoo tries to clarify his given name and surname (which the film's subtitles fail to translate as well). Unevenly entering the diegesis, the handheld translation device allows for only base-level communication between the characters, who join forces in a perfunctory manner. Although much remains untranslated between the characters, it doesn't seem to matter too much for characters who maintain discrete agendas.

We see a clear bifurcation between English- and Korean-speaking characters in the schoolroom scene, in which the teacher indoctrinates the children in the official version of the history of dissent on the train. As they pass the frozen figures that constituted the "Revolt of the Seven," she ends the story of the failed revolt with a clear moral. In a call-and-response format complete with quasi-fascist hand gestures, she leads the students in chanting: "If we ever go outside the train, we all freeze and die! If the engine stops running, we'd all die! And who takes care of the sacred engine? Go Wilford!" The Korean characters whisper a counterdiscourse in their language, which is crosscut with the teacher's disturbing pedagogy: "You look too. See over there. . . . That's a woman in the front. A cleaning lady from the front section. She was an Inuit. You know, Eskimo. She taught me every day about every type of snow and ice. She believed we could survive outside the train." The possibility of escape from the train is finally realized at the end of the film, but it is introduced in this schoolroom scene as contrary to the ideological indoctrination of the milieu and in the form of subtitled lines. As Curtis moves toward the front of the train, increasingly realizing that the revolution is a lie, that which is untranslated—outside of the diegesis and outside of the train—becomes the only alternative.

We see this tension most explicitly in the final conversation between Curtis and Minsoo, which isn't so much a conversation but rather a pair of sequenced soliloquies, with the would-be interlocutors only able to understand what the other is saying through affect and pantomime. Crucially here, the translation device is audible in the scene only at the beginning. It fades away and then becomes entirely inaudible, at which point the extradiegetic subtitles return. Each speaker offers a vision of what needs to be done next—Curtis wants to take control of the train, while Minsoo wants to get off it—but the imperfect translation at this would-be point of exchange means that the alternatives are not in conversation. Curtis begins with an account of his early experiences in the tail section, where he led a group of hungry men in killing weaker passengers to eat them. Cannibalism in the tail section is the flip side of the coin, the reverse of the violent population management initiated by the front of the train. Curtis speaks about Gilliam's amazing leadership in offering his own limbs to these men to save the children, a memory that establishes the frame for the later revelation that Curtis believes he is not fit for leadership because he still has his limbs. Curtis ends his speech by begging Minsoo to open the door to the engine room.

Expressing his alternative desire to open instead the door to the outside of the train, Minsoo takes his turn, noting observations he has made along the journey toward the front that suggest that it might again be possible to live outside: first, that a crashed airplane at the base of the Yekaterina Bridge, which had been covered with snow years ago, has become fully visible, suggesting that ice and snow have melted. His next observation, left incomplete, is one of the strangest moments in the film. He begins to tell Curtis about something he saw in the garden car, closing the loop from a moment earlier in the film when he is distracted by something he sees outside the window in the garden car. In contrast to Curtis's forward movements, Minsoo tends to move laterally in the film's blocking, suggesting his desire not to advance but to get off. Moving laterally in this earlier scene toward something off-screen, he had asked "What's that?" before the scene abruptly cut to the next car. Speaking now with Curtis, he begins to describe what he saw. We see a brief flashback to the memory in the garden car, but he stops short. Laughing it off, he says that there is no need to tell Curtis. Perhaps he believes that Curtis cannot understand his words, or that Curtis is too focused on getting to the engine. In any case, what Minsoo saw remains entirely outside of the diegesis. This is perhaps the point of this otherwise cryptic detail: that which is outside the train and outside the diegesis is aligned with that which is untranslated and thus remains outside the frame of reference as constituted by the train's imaginary. Though very little is articulated about the nature of what is outside the train, the very possibility of an outside as such is fetishized.

In *Snowpiercer*'s story about survival, translation marks both the point of potential logistical breakdown and the outside alternative that is otherwise wiped clear of the ideological framework of the train, which uses cultish leadership to maintain its fictions of sustainability. As a result, the vision of the outside remains ambivalent in the film. After the train wreck that ends the film, Yona emerges from the train with Tanya's son, Tim (Marcanthonee Reis), ostensibly the only survivors of the train and thus of humanity in general. They see a polar bear, which signals the possibility of renewed life on the planet, but perhaps only for a more resilient species. Far from utopian, the ending seems to suggest that the mere existence of an outside alternative in the context of a world that is confined to the space of the train is far easier to conceive of than the practical ways in which that alternative might manifest once it becomes a reality. Although the film ultimately seems to validate Minsoo's imperative to get off the train, it expends no resources to consider what this might mean beyond the simple fact of escape.[16] *Okja* too will end by satisfying a similar imperative; and though its representation of this outward escape seems a little less fantastical, it similarly falls short of utopian vision.

Fun Factory

Okja begins in a historical factory, where Lucy Mirando's grandfather long ago established the family's food empire. She has pointedly chosen this site for her inauguration as CEO of the Mirando Corporation, a global food conglomerate with subsidiaries in a host of related businesses, including fine dining supplies, baking, whole food, organic cosmetics, chemicals, and biotech. Wearing a luminescent white dress that contrasts sharply with the austere mise-en-scène of the rusting facility, she wishes to rupture rather than honor tradition (figure 15). She describes her grandfather as a "terrible man," and continues, "We know of the atrocities he committed in this space. We know these walls are stained with the blood of fine working men. But today, I reclaim this space to tell you a beautiful story. Now the rotten CEOs are gone. It's Mirando's new era with me, and with new core values, environment, and life. Awesome!" One journalist responds, "Oh, you're much more *fun* than the last chief executive."

Foregrounding the pivot toward this *fun* corporate strategy, the contrast between the drab industrial setting and Lucy's clean white dress is not coincidental. The snappy multimedia presentation and

Figure 15. Lucy Mirando wearing a white dress in
her family's old factory in *Okja*.

press conference are designed precisely to whitewash the legacy of a
historically suspect company. The inclusion of chemical manufacturing
as part of the corporate portfolio clues us into the inspiration for the
fictional Mirando Corporation—namely, the real American agricultural
and agrichemical conglomerate Monsanto, which was routinely derided
as one of the most evil corporations in the world before it was absorbed
into the German multinational Bayer in 2016. Among its many offenses,
Monsanto was responsible for introducing carcinogenic polychlorinated
biphenyls (PCBs) to the mass market in aspirin, despite knowledge of
their harmful effects (Gilliam). During wartime, it participated in the
development of weaponry, including uranium research for the Manhat-
tan Project during World War II and Agent Orange production during
the US war in Vietnam. It also developed and popularized toxic chemical
pesticides that found their way into the food supply. And, appropriately
for the present context, Monsanto was at the forefront of genetically
modified organisms (GMOs), not just in their production but also in
governmental lobbying. This last element of Monsanto's operations—its
brazen manipulation of legal and governmental oversite—was especially
widespread and pernicious. So powerful was Monsanto in the early
twenty-first century that its former lobbyist Islam Siddiqui could step
forward as the chief agricultural negotiator for the Trans-Pacific Partnership, a massive global trade pact that would have certainly advantaged
Monsanto had the United States not withdrawn from it in 2017.[17] Most
pertinently for *Okja*, Monsanto applied in 2005 under much controversy

for a patent for the "Monsanto Pig," and was granted it by the European Patent Office in 2008 (Peter).[18]

In this context, *Okja* updates for a new transnational marketplace E. B. White's classic children's novel *Charlotte's Web* (1952), which stages the pathos surrounding the story of a pig meant to become food. *Okja's* tale of a young girl's love for a genetically modified pig concerns itself, however, not just with the kind of global distribution of pork products imagined by Monsanto and echoed by Lucy Mirando but also with the distribution of another kind of global commodity, namely, movies. At this juncture in his career, Bong had just come off a contentious distribution arrangement for *Snowpiercer* with the Weinstein Company, which wanted to make significant cuts for the US release, causing the release to be significantly delayed. Bong lied, for example, that his father was a fisherman to convince Weinstein to keep the scene of Wilford's henchman cutting open the fish before the battle with Curtis's crew (Sharf). Seeking more control over distribution measures for his next film, Bong turned to Netflix and its hands-off approach for the global distribution of *Okja*. This was a controversial decision at the time because of the deleterious effect that many observers felt Netflix was having on the motion picture industry, not least for its practice of limited theatrical releases (or its avoidance of them altogether) in favor of its online streaming platform (Doo). Although the COVID-19 pandemic subsequently normalized simultaneous theatrical and online releases, circumstances were different in 2017, and *Okja* was booed at the Cannes Film Festival, both for the Netflix title card (a perceived violation of cinephile orthodoxy) and for a technical glitch at the top of the screening (Tiffany).

Splitting the phonic difference, then, between (Weinstein's) Miramax and Monsanto, Lucy's Mirando Corporation aims to proceed with its historical operations in food processing as if it were a global media conglomerate. Outlined in her grandfather's factory, Lucy's *fun* vision for the company uses media spectacle, celebrities, and heartwarming stories presented to a mass audience to cover over the vulgar world of slaughterhouses and genetic engineering at the heart of the family business. Bong's pairing of food and film production thus asks us to consider not just the processes through which commodities are made but also the means through which they are brought to market, tying its consideration of the ecological ramifications of global food sourcing to questions of global culture more broadly. What does a motion picture addressed to a global audience have to say about the cultures of globalized production and distribution?

In this multilayered context, *Okja* emerges as a story in which logistics are complicated not exactly by limited resources (as they were in *Snowpiercer*) but instead by a series of competing interests that all fixate on the same object. And unlike *Snowpiercer*, which reveals the ambiguity that emerges in a more-or-less binary class structure aboard the train (tail versus head), the struggle in *Okja* between the weak and powerful is complicated by a bumbling (but persistent) advocacy group, the Animal Liberation Front, which mediates the fight between the small-town Korean girl and the corporate giant, its good intentions creating chaos. In such an unstable milieu defined by complicated networks of competition, translation becomes important not as a strategy to circumscribe an alternative to ideological tunnel vision (as it was in *Snowpiercer*) but rather as a way to mark the inevitable entropy in all acts of competition and mediation. The ALF leader, Jay, is adamant about accurate translation, so much so that he beats K and banishes him from the group when he learns that K had intentionally mistranslated Jay's words to Mija, even though K had done so because of his profound devotion to the ALF mission.

Although most vigorously esteemed by Jay, the task of translation in the film is not exactly the utopian vision of seeking sympathetic reverberations between languages that Walter Benjamin once celebrated

Figure 16. Jay silently presenting a pretranslated message to Mija in *Okja*.

in Friedrich Hölderlin's translations of Sophocles: "the harmony of languages is so profound that sense is touched by language only the way an aeolian harp is touched by the wind" (262). Rather, translation in *Okja* is more instrumental, evocative of contractual consent and legal accord, notwithstanding the post-hippie lexicon that window-dresses the ALF's entreaties. To repair the mistrust resulting from K's original mistranslation, Jay appears silently in Mija's hotel room in New York, prepared with a message about the ALF's plan to rescue Okja, which he has had printed on a series of placards that he delivers sequentially (figure 16). Each one contains part of his message in English, with an accurate Korean translation printed below in easy-to-read text. Jay emotes with his face as he delivers the silent message to express his sincerity and to emphasize the one instruction that he wishes Mija to follow: not to look back at the screen when the ALF members leap into action. On the left-hand side of the screen next to Jay, we see an out-of-focus reflection of Mija in the mirror, reading the message as he presents it, a reflection that is doubled by more direct shots of Mija interspersed into the scene. The literal mirroring here represents the more figurative symmetry of accord that Jay wishes to achieve. We bear witness to translation as a kind of visual doubling. Not only are intentions clearly communicated with minimal interference—aside from the faint sounds of passing traffic and the rustling of the cards as Jay flips through them, this is a nearly soundless scene—the characters are presented as mirrored versions of each other: Paul wears the uniform of a bellhop as a disguise, while Mija holds the traditional Korean outfit (*hanbok*) that Lucy Mirando procured for her to wear for the event, an outfit that suits the caricature that Lucy wishes to present.

The emphasis on visual symmetry reflects the desire in this version of translation to achieve unambiguous agreement, which in turn reflects a broader desire in the film to manage the volatile nature of competition. But because the interests are triangulated in *Okja* between a multinational corporation, an international advocacy group, and a powerless foreign girl—as opposed to the simpler bifurcation in *Snowpiercer*—conflict becomes more diffuse. In addition to the ALF's war against corporate animal cruelty, Jay must manage dissent in his organization just as Lucy must hold at bay the advances of her more brutal twin sister, Nancy. Thus, not only do competing interests struggle for possession of Okja but power struggles also abound within each of the discreet interests. Even the singularly determined Mija must fight against the patriarchal plan for marriage envisioned by her grandfather, who opposes her desire to retrieve Okja. So, furthering the irony of *Snowpiercer*, in which revolutionary dissent is revealed to be coherent with corporate power, ideological antagonism in *Okja* becomes even more complicated. *Okja*'s allegorical staging of market competition as dramatic possession of a miracle pig, in which possession determines meaning (pig as food, symbol of corporate malfeasance, or beloved friend), fails to resolve into any clear determination and instead takes pleasure in the folly of any attempt to make sense of what at its core lacks any.

The world imagined in *Okja* is thus preposterous, emanating from the absurd conceit that a glut of pork products made from pigs genetically modified in a bleak New Jersey laboratory (and not raised naturally on a pastoral Chilean ranch as Lucy claims) might be marketed to an unsuspecting public as natural and organic. This is to say nothing about the fact that this hegemonic food corporation seems to ignore the largest pork market in the world (i.e., China) in its global strategy. Accordingly, the film is deeply parodic in its aesthetics. Full of performances that are either bombastic—like those of Tilda Swinton and Jake Gyllenhaal—or else caricatured and citational—like those of Paul Dano and Choi Woo-shik—the film crafts a world that becomes increasingly absurd and carnivalesque as it moves from the premodern terrain of the Korean countryside to the bustling American metropole where the film's climax takes place. Perhaps it is not just the pig in the film that is out of scale. Indeed, the very etymology of *parody*—with the Greek-derived prefix *par-* suggesting not only "alongside" and "beyond" but also "altered," "contrary," "irregular," and "abnormal" (*OED*)—seems to literalize in this context the logic of a GMO itself, which in turn finds its technological counterpart in *Okja* in the film's use of CGI. Produced by a visual effects team headed by Erik-Jan de Boer, the genetically modified eponymous pig in the film was represented during filming by a series of props that the team referred to as "stuffies," including a large suit (the pig) operated by a man standing inside of it, before the effect was digitally refined postproduction (Buder). As was the case with the CGI monster in *The Host*, the computer-generated spectacle in *Okja* represents its allegorical referent by exceeding it: the volatile colossus of empire in the former, the hubris of unchecked corporate ambition in the latter. GMO and CGI become twin technologies of excessive modification in *Okja*, both seeming to call for a parodic sensibility to express adequately the grotesque scale of monstrous technologies that, despite it all, lay claim to the real.

The implication of this unholy confluence of technological infringements on natural production is the insight that globalization tends toward parody, particularly as commerce becomes as much cultural as it is industrial, as in Lucy's vision for her company's multimedia pivot. Large-scale global enterprises (whether in the realm of global food processing or transnational media) require that their commodities shed their local particularity to become what Koichi Iwabuchi has described as the "culturally odorless" products of globalization (24–28). This removal of idiosyncratic marks that might diminish the range of their appeal along with the scaled-up scope of reproduction, however, not only entails the loss of aura caused by mechanical reproduction but also renders parody a more likely threat. The massively scaled reproducibility entailed by globalization inevitably yields unruly copies, which cannot help but mock original referents even as they recede from view.

Covered up by Lucy's fun, the real pivot in the film, then, is not between the old Mirando factory with its industrial modes of production and a cool media enterprise that deals in culture, but rather between the old factory and a new, even more brutal factory in which a vast, bleak field of genetically modified pigs are corralled one by one into a large mechanical contraption designed for efficient slaughter. In this context, Nancy is not just an antipodal alternative to her twin, the effervescent Lucy, but more precisely a mirror-reversed figure that reveals her sister's bubbly disposition as thin cover for a brutality that has persisted in Mirando all along. Here, with a quick mechanical twist, each pig is dispatched and sent down the assembly line, where workers transform their limp bodies into shrink-wrapped commodities. This becomes an appropriate site for the final vulgar transaction between Mija and Nancy Mirando, who has deposed her sister from leadership. Without the sentimental intervention of the "Some Pig" message inscribed on Charlotte's web to embarrass the underlying cruelty (White), Mija ultimately saves

Okja simply by paying for her with the pig made of solid gold that her grandfather gave her back in Korea, an exchange that Nancy is happy to make because for her Okja is no longer the focus of a transnational marketing campaign and simply another pig that she can exchange for something of greater value. The irony is that the gold pig was in fact purchased with money given to the grandfather for raising Okja. Nancy even bites the small pig to verify that it is indeed made of gold, a gesture that mimics the ingestion that will surely be the fate of all the actual pigs in the facility. The blunt relation of price to commodity here takes precedence over other forms of valuation, and the fixing of price in this scene comes to double the vision of translation as instrumental accord in the hotel room scene with Jay and Mija. In both cases, Mija comes to a functional agreement with the leader of a corporate entity—be it a revolutionary group or an actual corporation—while remaining indifferent to its motivations or nuances. That parties come to an understanding need not require that they understand each other.

If the aesthetics of *Okja* seem postmodern, it is because postmodernism is ultimately an expression of the late capitalist political economy that is the film's underlying logic. The film's devotion to parody in this context becomes more like pastiche, which Fredric Jameson describes as a "neutral practice" of the kind of mimicry that animates parody but without satiric "ulterior motives" (65), though, "as an inscription of the past in the present," it may retain the ability, according to Linda Hutcheon, "to embody and bring to life actual historical tension" (xii). Indeed, Jameson likens parody to a kind of translation, "speech in a dead language . . . devoid of laughter and of any conviction that alongside the abnormal tongue you have momentarily borrowed, some healthy linguistic normality still exists" (65). *Okja* thus homologizes global capital, rote translation, and empty parody; and it diagnoses the competing visions of the world imagined by Lucy and Jay as two versions of the same ambition, one in which repetition subsumes the requirements of basic social reproduction. The only way to turn the homogenizing tide is to escape its purview, though such escapes are less heroic than ambivalent. In *Snowpiercer*, to achieve escape outside of a totalizing system meant risking death to get off the crashing train. Less dramatically in *Okja*, it means returning to the remote mountain house for a home-cooked meal.

The Postfamily Dinner

The ending of *Okja* rehearses a motif that we witnessed first at the end of *The Host*—a family meal enjoyed by something resembling but not fully realizing a nuclear family. In the final scene of *The Host*, we see Gang-du sit down with the young boy he rescued from the monster, the same young boy that had been with Gang-du's daughter in her final days. Clicking off the television playing a news report about the events they themselves have directly experienced, they turn their attention to a Korean meal that Gang-du has prepared. The camera lingers while we watch them eat (they really dig in!), before we see the final shot, the snowy exterior of the store/home. This is of course not exactly a nuclear family: there remains no mother, and the father and son are not blood relations. But nevertheless, the family meal reminds us of this trope, less in the way of nostalgic longing and more as a provocation to imagine new forms of affiliation that would facilitate social reproduction, and perhaps without the ideological baggage. Similarly, the end of *Okja* is a Korean meal shared by Mija and her grandfather. Here the family transcends not bloodlines but species, with Okja visible in the far window, the baby pig they rescued from Mirando's pig farm lying down beside them. With her grandfather's back toward the camera, we see Mija take several bites before the film cuts to credits. In *Snowpiercer*, there is no meal (aside from the aborted steak dinner with Wilford and Curtis), but there is an improvised family of sorts with Yona and Tim, thrown together as postapocalyptic Adam and Eve, emerging from the wreckage of the train. Not instantly freezing to death as others had warned, they see a polar bear, which suggests that the earth might once again be able to sustain life.[19]

All three of these endings point toward possibilities of social reproduction outside of the oppressive systems that each film takes pains to detail. The meals and varied invocations of improvised familial relations collectively express a hope for such possibilities outside of the frameworks that come under critique in each successive film, be it US hegemony, postapocalyptic capitalism, or globalization. Appropriately, the physical setting of each of these scenes is remote. *The Host* situates us in a modest store on the banks of the Han River, abandoned by visitors for the winter. *Snowpiercer* takes us at last outside of the train, to a snowy valley in the mountains. *Okja* returns to Mija's remote village, far away from the New York offices of Mirando. And though the respective articulations of power in each film are clear eyed and canny, here in the endings the films seem instead to reach toward ideals that perhaps cannot bear much scrutiny. In imagining the outside of oppressive systems, these endings become almost necessarily naive, as if the task were not exactly to articulate the logistical details of a line of flight but simply to posit that one might exist.

Fantasies of Escape (Inside): *Parasite* (2019)

The endings of *Snowpiercer* and *Okja* depict escapes from oppressive systems that are accomplished by moving outside of them, though these escapes are more ambivalent than triumphant. By way of contrast, at the end of *Parasite*, Kim Ki-taek (Song Kang-ho) escapes the scene of his crime by fleeing *inside*. That is, after murdering Park Dong-ik (a.k.a. Nathan [Lee Sun-kyun]) at the garden birthday party for the Parks' son, relenting at last to the built-up resentment that Ki-taek has endured about his subordinate class status, Ki-taek runs down the staircase in front of the Parks' fancy house (the focus of the film) and toward the street. Instead of fleeing out toward the surrounding neighborhood, however, he turns back into the house and its secret basement bunker, the existence of which even the Parks are unaware. We might think of this decision as completing a figurative arc in the thematic trajectory explored in all of Bong Joon Ho's films, an arc that moves from earlier, locally rooted explorations of global influence on a national imaginary toward a more transnational vision of global engagement (see D. H. Kim 45). These opposing orientations fold back in on themselves in *Parasite*, a film that is conflicted about how to situate its own story. Thus, the escape inside the house is not exactly a regressive retreat into familiar or nostalgic complacencies. Rather, the mise-en-scène of the house becomes a mise en abyme in which the house is a miniature version of the world it expresses. It is not that the return inside the house refuses the globalized world; it is that the globalized world has become fully internalized in the logic of the house.

Thus, on the one hand, *Parasite* prioritizes a domestic sensibility that implies the sanctity of nationhood. *Parasite* was inspired in part by Kim Ki-young's classic film *The Housemaid*, a film set primarily in a two-story house that functioned as an allegory for a modernizing Korea. On the other hand, not only is the Parks' lovely house the site of intense competition, in which upstarts might wrest control over the domestic space from others, this competition is also revealed to be determined by a set of transnational relations, which the film invokes through Cold War tropes, most prominently the bunker built for the event of a North Korean attack, and the film's Native American imagery, which links the plot of domestic occupation to the US history of settler colonialism in its expansionary phase (see J. J. Jeon, "Lines"). Thus, if the house in *Parasite* figures the nation, it is under very different conditions than those encountered by Kim Ki-young. From one of the poorest nations in the world in the immediate postwar period, South Korea developed into one of the world's wealthiest nations by the end of the twentieth century. And though it never threatened US global hegemony as Japan did in the 1980s, South Korea became a semi-imperial power with its own growing network of value chains extending into the Global South, particularly in Southeast Asia. The exploding popularity of Korean popular culture around the world—epitomized by K-pop acts like BTS and Blackpink, Korean television shows like *Squid Game* (2021) and *Crash Landing on You* (2019), and indeed the films of Bong Joon Ho—was a signature of this growing influence, but at the same time threatened to dilute its distinctiveness as Korean entertainment companies attempted to appeal to broader audiences. In 2023, for example, it was reported that 90 percent of K-pop listeners reside outside of South Korea (Yoon). At the time of writing, *Parasite* is the most globally successful Korean movie of all time, and its focus on domestic spaces begs fundamental questions about its nature. In the overdetermined space of the Parks' beautiful modernist house, then, *Parasite* tries to make sense of a historical moment in which the impulse to expand outward for growth opportunities encounters its limit. The only remaining option, a fantasy to be sure, is to escape inside. Where global engagement may once have offered opportunities, the belated realization here is that with such prospects come considerable vulnerabilities. The inward line of flight, however, is something more vexed than a backslide into ethnonationalism; rather, it figures an impasse at which global competition is both desired and feared and in which the compulsion toward expansionary growth becomes an object of dread not least because it seems the only available option.

Given this broad historical framework invoked by *Parasite*, it is worth reflecting on the film as a cultural phenomenon, epitomized by its unexpected win at the 2020 Academy Awards for Best Picture—the first foreign-language film to take the prize—which followed its equally historic win of the Palme d'Or at the 2019 Cannes Film Festival, the first Korean film ever to win the prestigious festival's top prize. The film's success, however, is a little less surprising when we recognize that the film was produced within the purview of US historical logics (see Moon and Moon). South Korea was a key client state in the postwar US-centered world system, which shifted in the 1990s into the economic imperium known as the Washington Consensus (see Held).[20] Both a system of global trade and an economic philosophy, the Washington Consensus was organized around global market liberalization, privatization, and a host of economic policy prescriptions that have coalesced under the rubric of *neoliberalism* (see Harvey, "Neo-Liberalism").[21] Despite its salutary "global village" branding, this arrangement came to dominate global commerce. Although it emerged out of postwar liberal internationalism, the Washington Consensus was more aggressive and demanding, designed as it was to maintain US hegemony past the point at which the United States could provide the engine for global economic growth.[22] The Washington Consensus implemented its dominance frequently through postwar Bretton Woods institutions like the IMF, which infamously extracted a horrific set of concessions from South Korea as part of the bailout package during the 1997–98 Asian financial crisis (see Wade and Veneroso; Cumings). Although it came to an end with the failure of the US-led Trans-Pacific Partnership in 2017, the Washington Consensus had persisted through the millennium, facilitating the increasingly extractive strategies of US hegemony even as it fell short of promised benefits.[23] But by the time of *Parasite*'s triumph at the Oscars, which coincided with a wave of antiglobalist, protectionist bravado (epitomized by but not limited to the Trump administration), the era of the Washington Consensus had ended, leaving export-dependent economies like that of South Korea in the lurch.

In this context, the Parks' house represents not just a nation that is contained within a single household but also the irritated relationship between that more contained figure and the networked global systems in which that house is inevitably situated. It is no surprise, then, that domestic space in the film becomes vulnerable to invasion and ultimately violence, however shielded it might initially seem by wealth. Although representations of structural inequality along class lines have a long and rich history in Korean film, what is distinctive about *Parasite*'s treatment of this familiar theme has to do with the material conditions that have recently come to underlie the Korean political economy, at a time when the growth rates of this decidedly export-oriented economy have hovered at the threshold for secular stagnation, causing a good deal of consternation about the limits of the domestic frame (see Summers; Cooper, "Secular"; Brouillette et al.). Although the fact of the Parks' wealth is incontrovertible, what does come into question is the ability of this wealth to sustain a broader system of dependents in the manner that Korean family-owned corporations (*chaebol*) had once done, cultivating a thriving middle class during the nation's developmental period, when the Korean economy was hailed as the Miracle on the Han. In those earlier years, a rapid industrial boom required a robust labor pool that was made possible by high growth rates, and thus the system promised lifetime employment for workers, who were ideologically framed as part of the family (Cumings 64).

But with those heady days in the rearview mirror, the decades since the 1990s proved more challenging while also auguring future difficulties. Threats posed by an aging population, low birth rates, and increased competition in key industries (particularly from China) became worrisome, especially as South Korea's historical alliance with the United States became increasingly vexed. These and other facts combined to produce a sense of haunting vulnerability that persisted alongside spectacles of wealth for Korean elites. An important backdrop for *Parasite*, skyrocketing real estate prices in Seoul made the dream of home ownership indeed a fantasy for many young Koreans (see Wagner), but larger political economic frames became even more pertinent. Japanese "lost decade" stagnation beginning in the 1990s seems prescient, as South Korea struggled to shift to an alternative model for sustained growth after its rapid industrial expansion (see Harris). In this context, we see that the film's explicit concern for class inequality is deepened by the lack of overall economic growth.[24] Characters fight for their piece of the pie precisely because there is not enough to go around. We might say more generally that stories of class difference take on a pointedly different tenor during periods of stagnation; the anxiety in *Parasite* is not just over the moral fact of social inequality but also about the equitable distribution of wealth in the face of diminishing resources. Brutal competition emerges from a milieu that is only ostensibly defined by plentitude, and the agon of the film is not just between rich and poor, but also between poor and poor. The Parks' lavish house thus figures Korean class relations not just because it so starkly contrasts with the impoverishment of the Kims' half-basement dwelling but also because it is presented, despite its opulence, as a limited space in which all occupants must compete for control in zero-sum fashion to survive the difficulties of contemporary life.

In this respect, it is clarifying to note that the house is in some profound respects virtual (see K. H. Kim, *Virtual* 1–21). That is, it does not exist as a freestanding house anywhere but rather is a combination of studio sets in different locations, which were in turn augmented by visual effects. As was revealed in an article appropriately published in *Architectural Digest*, the first floor and garden were built in an empty lot, with CGI used to represent the second floor for exterior shots; the interior scenes set on the second floor along with the basement scenes were shot on a separate soundstage (Wallace). At the same time, to fill out the mise-en-scène, the sets for the house were incredibly detailed, with no expense spared to fill them with credible opulence, including real (valuable) art pieces by the Korean artist Seung-mo Park and a trash can for the kitchen that purportedly cost $2,300 (Wallace; E. A. Jung). Bong even created detailed backstories for the unseen characters (including an old woman who makes her living by recycling garbage and a wannabe YouTuber) who occupy the homes in the neighborhood surrounding the Kims' half-basement home, which was built in a water tank that could be flooded and inspired by soon-to-be-destroyed, empty towns in Korea visited by set designer Lee Ha-jun (Wallace). The virtuality of the mise-en-scène in turn underwrites the malleability with which it takes on meaning in the film, particularly as the house comes to be regarded as the site of competition.

Ultimately, the virtuality of the house in *Parasite* goes along with its function as a kind of *gamespace*, or, as McKenzie Wark has glossed, "a world of pure agon, of competitive striving after distinction" (5). As such, the generic invocations of competition narratives remind us, as have critics like Wark, that the late capitalist sensibility that *Parasite* exemplifies has become gamified to the extent that it has become more intensely competitive, or as Wark puts it: "Agony rules! Everything has value only when ranked against something else; everyone has value only when ranked against someone else. . . . Games are no longer a pastime, outside or alongside of life. They are now the very form of life, and death, and time itself" (6).

To express this kind of intense competition, *Parasite* situates in its gamespace a pair of genres that have become more prominent in contemporary film and television, the confidence game and the battle royal.[25] While both are suffused with the playfulness of games and emphasize tactical maneuvers, they are ultimately very different in tone. Put simply, whereas the confidence game tends toward comedy, battle royal tends toward horror. By moving from the lighthearted genre to its more brutal cousin, the film tracks the stakes of the broader historical transitions it maps in late globalization, when postwar structures of international cooperation sour under the force of intensified competition. Within this shifting generic orientation, the film's allegorical depictions of a poor family's exploitation of a wealthy family's service needs become a means to track the geopolitical dependencies that have characterized postwar South Korean history leading up to the juncture in the first decades of the twenty-first century, when it finds itself staggering as the ground shifts beneath its feet.

Confidence *Kyehoek*

The film's plot begins in the generic manner of a confidence game, depicting the logistically intensive machinations of the Kims as they contrive to take over all the service positions in the Parks' household, displacing the existing staff. Here the film is comic, with the characters repressing the knowledge that the boon to their family well-being comes at the expense of those that they displace. In the film's first act, we see the Kims successively plotting, rehearsing, and then enacting their cleverly improvised plan to gain employment for the entire family, beginning with Ki-woo (a.k.a. Kevin [Choi Woo-shik]), who gets hired as the tutor for the Parks' daughter on the recommendation of a friend. Ki-woo in turn recommends his sister, Ki-jung (a.k.a. Jessica [Park So-dam]), whom he passes off as an expert art teacher and child therapist with a considerable reputation. Ki-jung then takes advantage of an earnest miscalculation by the Parks' driver to frame him as a pervert, and subsequently recommends Ki-taek for the job, without acknowledging the kinship. The final and most elaborate element of the con is to depose the family's housekeeper, who had worked for the original owner and designer of the house, an architect named Namgoong, which is incidentally also the name for Song Kang-ho's character in *Snowpiercer*. They replace her with Chung-sook, completing the scheme to get all four of the Kim family members into the employment of the Parks while hiding their familial relation.

In this long first act of the film, the viewer becomes swept up in the Kims' playful logistics and daring machinations, some of which they explicitly rehearse, complete with written scripts, in the manner of mise en abyme, as if preparing to act in a dramatic performance. The audience is encouraged to bracket off consequences to participate in the pleasures of complicated plans executed with precision and creativity. At one point, in a moment of self-reflexivity, Ki-woo speculates that the family's previous driver (who was framed as a degenerate by Ki-jung) must be doing fine, with his youth and good looks intact, thus calling attention to the way in which the genre downplays the harm caused by the plan. As exemplified in Hollywood classics like *The Sting* (1973) and *Ocean's Eleven* (1960, 2001) and in Korean heist movies like *The Thieves* (*Todukdŭl*, 2012), the confidence game narrative buoyantly encourages cathexis with charismatic criminals, inviting audiences to take pleasure in cunning gameplay while setting aside darker associations of criminality. The added layer in *Parasite* is that the pleasure of the scheme is doubled by the spectacle of a happy nuclear family, its members working industriously in harmonious unity toward their shared goal of prosperity, a vision that stands in ironic contrast to the deceitful means through which they achieve their goals.[26]

Even in the first scenes in the film, before the larger confidence game begins, we see the Kims engaged in smaller-scale versions of improvised plotting to survive daily life. In the very first scene of the film, the children discover that the Wi-Fi they have been poaching from the neighbor upstairs has become password protected. Assessing the problem of their deactivated phone services, Chung-sook kicks Ki-taek, who is napping on the floor, to ask him what his *plan* is. The scene immediately cuts to a shot of a photograph mounted on the wall of Chung-sook in a hammer-throw competition, alongside the silver medal that she won in that event. This trope of Olympic-style games is repeated later in the film in Geun-sae's (Park Myung-hoon) shrine, which includes a few semi-famous silver medal–winning Korean athletes. The Korean word Chung-sook uses is *kyehoek* (plan or scheme), which is used repeatedly by the family throughout the course of the film. Ki-taek tells the children to seek out another Wi-Fi signal by holding their phones high in the air, and they eventually locate one that is accessible only from the elevated toilet platform in the bathroom. The juxtaposition of Ki-taek's *kyehoek* and Olympic-style games frames the many schemes in the film as located somehow not in the real world but in a kind of fictive gamespace in which competition has only limited consequences because the competition is imagined as occurring within these circumscribed limits.

In a subsequent scene, even labor is understood in these gamified terms. The Kims work together in folding a large pile of pizza boxes for a local shop, seeking guidance from a YouTube video posted by a particularly talented box folder. And when the proprietor of the pizza shop balks on payment because of the poor quality of the work, Ki-woo steps in with some gamesmanship of his own, angling for an unlikely job at her shop, perhaps with the intuition that her unwillingness to hire him will cause her to relent and pay the family to avoid a larger imbroglio. It is no wonder then that an initial gambit for the Kims' deception of the Parks occurs in a PC bang, a public space that young Koreans typically use to blow off steam and play video games, often to escape the pressures of their high-stakes education (figure 17; see Se-young Kim 136). Here, with adolescents playing video games all around her (mostly first-person shooters), Ki-jung plays a different sort of game, masterfully forging university documents on behalf of her brother, Ki-woo, who will soon present them as credentials for employment. Smoking a cigarette against the rules of the establishment, Ki-jung initially seems anomalous in the space, working as she is on her forgery on behalf of her brother's larger deception. But in the generic context of the confidence plot, her efforts performed in a space that is literally associated with gaming reflect the larger orientation of the

Figure 17. Ki-jung forging university documents
for Ki-woo at a PC bang in *Parasite*.

Kims toward the agon of Wark's gamespace, in which the imperative
of competition trumps any rules of social propriety.

These recursive breaches of social and legal decorum are autho-
rized for the Kims by the need to merely survive. Thus, the family's
confidence *kyehoek* perpetrated against the Parks under the erratic
orchestration of Ki-taek becomes understood as an extension of many
years of extemporized economic struggle, struggle that has taken the
form of a series of jobs and failed family businesses, including Ki-taek's
job as a valet parking attendant, investment in a fried chicken shop, and
the opening of a Taiwanese cake shop (see *Wall Street Journal*). This
prehistory of the Kim family helps distinguish their long con from the
classic Hollywood archetype. Rather than angling for a big score, the
confidence *kyehoek* here aims for a more modest goal: the avoidance of
destitution. In this regard, the disparity between the heights of success
and the likely fate ensured by the plan's failure implies a similar dynamic
as those of what I have described elsewhere as *subsistence faming* (J. J.
Jeon, *Vicious* 75–76). Well suited to describing the experiences of K-pop
aspirants (the vast majority of whom fail, despite their commitment to
intense and prolonged training regimes that are highly monitored by
handlers), *subsistence faming* implies conditions in which one must
achieve spectacular success to avoid abject poverty, with little to no safety
net in between. Although the Kims do not aspire for fame per se, the
all-or-nothing character of their enterprise reproduces these conditions.
The audaciousness of the Kims' confidence *kyehoek* ultimately expresses
the gravity of their desperation.

(Deadly Serious) Battle Royal

The confidence *kyehoek* encompasses the entirety of the film's first act, culminating with a drunken party that the Kims hold in the Parks' living room while the Parks are away on a camping trip. The film, however, executes a tonal heel turn the moment that the former housekeeper, Moon-gwang (Lee Jung-eun), rings the doorbell. This pivot from comedy to horror is foreshadowed earlier during the Parks' party, when Chung-sook teases her husband, intimating that he would flee like a cockroach if Mr. Park were to suddenly walk into the house. Seeming to take offense at the insulting comparison, Ki-taek violently clears the table with a swipe of his arm, sending bottles and glasses crashing to the floor. He grabs his wife by the shirt, threatening her with a menacing glare. After a long tense pause, they both begin to giggle, with Chung-sook realizing that Ki-taek has acted in jest. Humor alleviates the tension, but the surprise violence of the joke's reckless setup nevertheless lingers. The scene toggles so quickly between comedy and horror that they seem to become momentarily opposite sides of one coin. This toggling between comedy and horror inheres in one of the film's most iconic lines, a moment of unintentional comedy when Park matriarch Yeon-gyo (Cho Yeo-jeong) tells Ki-jung in English, "I'm deadly serious," in response to a question about her interest in the driver Ki-jung has mentioned. Yeon-gyo is fond of sprinkling English phrases into her speech (a particularly Korean bourgeois peccadillo) despite her lack of overall fluency, and thus repeatedly produces discordant moments like this one, uncannily comic (particularly for global audiences), which ironically make light of a solemnity worthy of death.

The hint of this relation between comedy and horror becomes fully realized upon Moon-gwang's arrival, and especially when she brings Chung-sook and the audience with her into the house's secret basement, where her husband has been living for years. Here, the Kims are presented with a figure who has suffered from their fun confidence game; we see Moon-gwang feeding Geun-sae with a baby bottle, a heavy-handed image meant to convey his vulnerability. It is at this point that the frame shifts toward battle royal, as the confidence game's cool operations reveal their harsh stakes and foreshadow the violent killings to come in the film's second half. But more than simply shifting the generic coordinates from one to the other, *Parasite* in this transition suggests the deep connection between the confidence game and battle royal, which it implicitly links under the rubric of competition. Indeed, battle royal raises the stakes of the confidence game by connecting success to survival, against the statistically more likely outcome of death. Perhaps because it is so inherently inhospitable to human thriving, battle royal tends to morph into other generic forms, most commonly narratives of escape (*Death Race*, 2008) or of revolution (*The Hunger Games*, 2012). The most relevant context here might be Japanese *sabaibukei*, or survival fictions, which emerged around the turn of the century, as most famously exemplified by Takami Kōshun's *Batoru rowaiyaru* (*Battle Royale*, 1999). The genre has been read as a reaction to the endless recession and unstable social situation of the period, creating a good deal of anxiety particularly in Japanese youth, whose prospects became radically circumscribed (Tanaka).[27] Crucially, both confidence games and battle royal suspend moral considerations and displace them with more pressing concerns—logistics in the confidence game, survival in battle royal—such that violent spectacles become rationalized by stressful circumstances. While the latter may be regarded as blunter, both subgenres invoked in *Parasite* represent brutal competition in the social milieu of contemporary Korean society, which defines success (and indeed survival) as necessarily coming at someone else's expense, whether that be through the clever dispossession in the con game or cold slaughter in the manner of battle royal.

Both also foreground contained, gamified spaces to demarcate moral suspension.[28] The confidence plot tends to dilate on a protected structure that is to be infiltrated, like a bank, casino, or racetrack. Battle royal is even more pronounced in its spatial aesthetics, foregrounding a defined and highly mediated (often televised) arena of contestation for the violent competition, like an island or prison.[29] In *Parasite*, the house serves both functions. When the tables turn on the Kim family after Moon-gwang and Geun-sae discover their machinations and the power dynamic swings wildly, it happens in the living room, still littered with the remains of the earlier party. The Kims are forced to kneel on the floor with their hands in the air as Moon-gwang and Geun-sae luxuriate on the couch, threatening to send an incriminating video to the Parks that would expose the Kims' deceit. During this scene, Geun-sae begins to reminisce about happy times the couple spent in the house when free from the observation of its proprietors. The scene cuts to a shot of Moon-gwang and Geun-sae in the same room, furnished differently to emphasize the temporal shift, listening and dancing to pleasant music on the record player with sunlight bathing the room in splendor. We cut then to a shot of the couple drinking tea on the couch out of fine china, looking out the window. Just in time to see the surprise attack, Geun-sae turns toward the camera, and we see Chung-sook leading her family in a charge toward Moon-gwang and Geun-sae (figure 18). This is a remarkable scene because it connects disparate temporalities, as if the Kims were taking this moment of pleasurable memory to attack not just their antagonists but also the memory itself. We learn from this heterochronic staging—in which one family seems to attack the other from a different temporal dimension—that the competition for

Figure 18. Moon-gwang and Geun-sae turning toward the camera in anticipation of the attack by the Kims from a different temporality in *Parasite* (*above*). Chung-sook leading her family in their attack on Moon-gwang and Geun-sae in *Parasite* (*below*).

the house in *Parasite* involves more than just a fight for who gets to enjoy its pleasures. Beyond its material attributes, the house also affords its residents a fantasy of separation from the brutal world of competition that seems to define life outside of it. But over the course of the film, as is presaged in this scene, this fantasy becomes impossible to sustain, even for those most thickly insulated by wealth.

The physical struggle in the living room between the two families who had been engaged in a tactical struggle for service jobs in the Park household, which ends with the death of Moon-gwang and the incarceration of Geun-sae back in the subterranean bunker, anticipates the even larger melee that happens in the yard in the plain light of day during the garden party. In retrospect, the violence that erupts at the party might come as no surprise given its thematic orientation toward disparate forms of colonial violence. Yeon-gyo instructs Chung-sook to arrange the tables around Da-song's (Jung Hyeon-jun) Native American tepee in the manner of Admiral Yi Sun-shin's crane wing formation, with the tepee as the Japanese warship and the party tables forming a semicircular crane wing.[30] The reference is to the military tactics of the legendary sixteenth-century admiral who successfully defended Korea from a Japanese attack at the Battle of Hansan Island, where he employed the formation that Yeon-gyo appropriates for her party. Furthermore, for the party's main event, Nathan Park plans a mock Indian attack for his son, with himself and Ki-taek dressed in feathered headdresses, serving as the Native American assailants. Although it is more a set of empty signifiers, a childhood preoccupation that is ultimately oblivious to the history of settler colonial genocide it implies, the Native American imagery in the garden party in the context of Korean-Japanese warfare becomes reendowed with its original historical meaning. The Native American iconography of the film (tepees and headdresses) is specifically that of Plains tribes like the Lakota, which first captured the American imagination after the defeat of General George Custer and US forces at the Battle of the Little Bighorn (1876), during a period of violent conflict between an expansionary United States and the Native tribes that opposed the appropriation of their territories. It is no wonder then that the historically overdetermined garden party ends in violent bloodshed.

The garden party in the yard also marks the moment when Ki-taek in particular seems to acknowledge that the competition depicted in the film does not just occur between the two poor families but includes the wealthy one as well. The scene begins to turn from festive to morose when Geun-sae emerges from the basement with knife in hand. After a beat to let his eyes adjust to the sunlight, he makes a beeline for Ki-jung, stabbing her in the chest as she instinctively smashes the birthday cake she had been holding into his face. The combination of the timeless slapstick trope (classically pies in the face, not cakes) and the brutal murder returns us to the film's toggling between comedy and horror. The revenge sought by Geun-sae for the killing of his wife and more broadly for the Kims' rude interruption of his strangely happy life in the Parks' basement becomes in this moment an austere rejoinder to the confidence plot's callous avoidance of the plot's victims. After Ki-jung falls to the ground, Geun-sae turns his attention to Chung-sook, whom he calls out by name, and they engage in fighting that ends when Chung-sook stabs him in the side with a barbeque skewer that still has some shrimp and hot dogs speared on it up toward the hilt. Shortly thereafter, Nathan Park uses the skewer as a lever to roll Geun-sae over to get his car keys, which had been thrown underneath the man's body.

It is at this moment, specifically when Nathan reacts in disgust to Geun-sae's foul odor, that Ki-taek snaps and finally recognizes Nathan Park as an antagonistic competitor in Ki-taek's struggle for his family's survival rather than a source of opportunity. Ki-taek had largely viewed employment in the Park household as a boon, even entertaining the fantasy that his son might marry the Parks' daughter. This view is challenged throughout the film when, for one reason or another, Ki-taek's scent becomes a topic of notice, initially when Da-song observers that the family's new employees all smell the same. Later reflecting on the problem, Ki-jung disabuses her parents of the belief that the smell comes from the laundry detergent that Chung-sook uses to clean their clothes; rather, she says, it comes from their half-basement apartment. The scent, in other words, is that of poverty.[31] The odor becomes stronger on the morning of the garden party, which comes a day after a storm that had brought the Parks home early from camping and flooded the Kims' half-basement apartment with sewage water while they tried in vain to save their belongings. Yeon-gyo notices it from the back seat of the car with Ki-taek driving. She opens the window without openly reprimanding Ki-taek, but he notices and is humiliated by her reaction. Thus, when

Ki-taek notices Nathan Park revolting at the smell of Geun-sae even as Geun-sae expends his dying words to express his admiration for Mr. Park, Ki-taek snaps and takes the knife from where it fell on the ground to stab his employer in the chest. Up to this point, the violence of the scene had been structured by revenge: Geun-sae attacks Ki-jung to avenge his wife's killing, after trying to kill Ki-woo in the basement (though Ki-woo recovers). Chung-sook in turn kills Geun-sae as a response to the killing of Ki-jung. These acts of vengeance are an extension of the competition the two families have engaged in throughout the film, but Ki-taek's attack on Nathan Park marks a turning point in his view of his employer and the house's current proprietor, a recognition of Nathan Park as part of and not exterior to the brutal competition that the film has staged throughout its duration. As in all zero-sum competitions, in the end there are no affiliations to be preserved in battle royal.

Editing Inside/Out

After the violence at the garden party and after Ki-taek has fled the scene only to circle back inside the house and into the safety of the basement bunker, the film attempts to return abruptly to the comic mode with which it began. Ki-woo cannot stop laughing upon regaining consciousness from his head trauma, prompted initially by the sight of a police officer who does not look like a police officer, who is trying to read Ki-woo his Miranda rights, next to a doctor who does not look a doctor, who is explaining Ki-woo's laughter in medical terms to the officer. His compulsive laughter continues through his trial and even a visit to Ki-jung's memorial site, but it ends when he later watches the news reports of the garden party killings. After one more comic pratfall by a detective trailing Ki-woo down a flight of stairs, the film abandons comic pursuits to focus on Ki-woo's discovery back at the Parks' house, now occupied by another family, of a Morse code message from his father, whom Ki-woo learns is holed up in the house's secret basement bunker, as Geun-sae had been before him. Ki-woo sees the message (conveyed through a flickering light) after visiting the hill above the house and for some undeclared reason watching it through a pair of binoculars.

On the night Ki-woo notices the Morse code message from Ki-taek, we see the new residents of the house (we learn from Ki-taek's message that they are a German family) through the living room's floor-to-ceiling

Figure 19. Fade cut inside but not outside the house in *Parasite*.

windows. We see five figures moving about the couch, including a house-keeper who brings the family refreshments from the kitchen as another female figure moves toward the kitchen (we catch a glimpse of her moving form in the smaller side window). At this moment, there is a fade cut to a moment slightly later in the evening, and we see the family's father and the housekeeper disappear from their initial positions on and near the couch. At the same time, the father fades into view as he approaches the window to look outside. For a brief moment, fade cutting to a slightly later moment, the father's form on the couch appears simultaneously with his form in front of the window (figure 19).

But crucially here, the cut only occurs inside, not outside, the house. We know this because the steadily falling snowflakes continue outside without interruption in their path toward the ground at the precise moment that the cut occurs inside. The scene thus enacts a strange temporal disjuncture between the temporality of inside and outside. It disjunctively advances time to a slightly later moment via the cut inside, while the natural image of snow falling acts as an index of the continuous timeline proceeding outside. Time is indeed out of joint. At the same time, the fading and reemerging image of the German father reminds us of the other father, Ki-taek, trapped in the basement below the house and locked in a time loop of his own, able only to recursively send his Morse code message to his son without ever knowing whether his son will receive the transmission.

We might think of this moment in relation to the paired use of mise-en-scène and mise en abyme in the *Mother* prison scene with which we began this study. The mise-en-scène of the drab state institution suggested both the private torture experienced by the mother and the torque placed on her conscience toward social responsibility. Subsequently, the visual mise en abyme, with its suggestion of endless mirroring, the paradoxical expansion and contraction of space, implied the reverberating impact of her refusal to honor social responsibility to the community immediately around her—for which the falsely accused man served as a figure—and beyond it to the broader social structure in which that community is embedded. In a similar manner in *Parasite*, we are presented within the context of a singular structure, a fancy modernist house, with a series of disjunctions that encourages us to see that singular location instead via the complex set of relations that flow through it, to see, that is, a private space as instead one of social conflict and competition, with ultimately global implications. Apropos of a milieu in which cops don't look like cops, and doctors don't look like doctors, we are forced to shed our assumptions and seek alternative frames of reference.

In the cut that occurs inside and not outside the house, we are offered an image of asymmetrical time that connotes a series of reversals: a former insider who has been cast outside (Ki-woo can only observe from afar) and a globalized system that has infiltrated domestic terrain (Germans in a once-Korean-owned house). Realigning expectations, the Korean perspective manifested by Ki-woo now views the domestic space from an external position while the domestic interior is ironically occupied by foreigners. This is to say nothing of the Korean man ensconced in the basement out of view, feebly signaling his presence with only a blinking light. The temporal asymmetry of the relations in this shot—the discontinuity between time inside the house, outside of it, and below it—offers then a still more nuanced form of the transnational comparative perspective detailed by Raymond Williams at the end of *The Country and the City*, but here the colony and metropole become more interchangeable. The German man, Ki-woo, and Ki-taek are all actors in the relation depicted in this scene, but they occupy different temporalities even though they coincide in proximate spaces. Only Ki-woo, positioned at a distance, can begin to articulate the terms of this relation, while the German man and Ki-taek are entirely oblivious.

Coda: Mise en mondial

A once-domestic space, the house at the end of *Parasite* is thus fully realized as a global one, resting on a foundation of Cold War histories and with the figural positions of natives and foreigners reversed with respect to the boundaries of the house. There are layered implications in this spatial arrangement, in which mise-en-scène and mise en abyme come to overlap as the film's plot of combined and uneven development reveals its underlying complexities. In this respect, the house fully realizes what is only latent in the dynamic of the jail visiting room in *Mother*, where the sense of tortured confinement radiates outward into a larger echo chamber. The multivalent layers of the home at the end of *Parasite* ultimately reflect a post–Washington Consensus political economy, in which domestic control has been ceded to external forces, worrying the problem of how to take back control of the house. Here, the concern is for the relative agency of South Koreans in a rapidly transitioning landscape. In this respect, it might be said that contemporary South Korea has much in common with present-day Germany as an economically powerful but not hegemonic nation that is increasingly dependent on China as a market for its exports but atavistically dependent on the United States for its security (Ebbighausen). As the Washington Consensus further dissolves, this becomes an increasingly untenable position. This geopolitical precarity leads in turn to another layer, the gradual evanescence of the United States from this picture of the global. As Michelle Cho has reminded us, what "global" meant before the current moment of globalization was simply "American" ("K-Crossover"). By the time of *Parasite*'s release, however, this was no longer the case. Although the secret foundation of the house in *Parasite* remains associated with the Cold War, with which the United States of course remains very much associated in the Korean context, it is striking to note that the film offers a more complicated picture of the global, as befitting a world that is pivoting away from its twentieth-century axioms and becoming far more opaque in the process.

In this context, the rendering of the house at the end of *Parasite* as Ki-woo looks at it from afar self-reflexively seems also to ask about the nature of a Korean cultural product aimed at the evolving global marketplace. Given the need for broad appeal, how Korean do these products remain? To what extent are Koreans left on the outside looking in? This is a question also begged by Bong's subsequent film, *Mickey 17* (2025), a transnational production starring the British Hollywood actor Robert Pattinson. Although the film has not been released at the time of writing, I would like to position it, in closing this study, as the horizon toward which this study has progressed, based not only on what we know of its plot but also, and more importantly, on the specific conditions of its emergence, in relation both to the trajectory of Bong Joon Ho's career as I have outlined it in this book and to twenty-first-century global filmmaking writ large. My hope is that these speculations might provoke compelling questions about the film itself as well as provide a useful roadmap for future encounters with Bong's work and its evolving global entanglements.

The first film produced by Bong Joon Ho after *Parasite*, *Mickey 17* is an English-language feature film made with a predominantly Western cast. Although he was also developing at the same time a Korean-centered project, an animated film about deep-sea creatures whose production began in 2024, it is notable that the more global project was produced first and released most immediately after the meteoric success of *Parasite*. Based on a 2022 sci-fi novel by Edward Ashton, *Mickey 17* tells the story of Mickey Barnes, a "disposable" employee on a space expedition to colonize an ice planet. Mickey is disposable in the sense that he regularly undertakes extremely dangerous work, in which death is a likely and in fact frequent outcome. Mickey has died sixteen times prior to the time frame of the film, which tells the story of his seventeenth iteration. As a precaution, his memories are stored prior to each assignment; in the event of death, these memories are uploaded into a cloned body so that Mickey can continue to live his life, if only in this strange, uncanny manner (figure 20).

Distributed by the storied Hollywood studio Warner Bros. and shot at the studio's facility in Leavesden, England, *Mickey 17* is the closest that Bong Joon Ho has come to working within a Hollywood framework and its material conditions. Indeed, the film's initial scheduled release in March 2024 had to be significantly postponed due to production delays caused by the 2023 SAG-AFTRA (Screen Actors Guild–American Federation of Television and Radio Artists) strike. Just as *Snowpiercer* starred actor Chris Evans after his performance as Captain America in a series of

Figure 20. Shot of Robert Pattinson as Mickey in
Mickey 17.

Marvel Studios productions, *Mickey 17* stars Robert Pattinson fresh off
his performance in *The Batman* (2022), though Pattinson was also not far
removed from a celebrated sci-fi turn in global art cinema in Claire Denis's
High Life (2018). One wonders nevertheless whether Ki-woo remains
nestled in the hills peering through his binoculars, perhaps a little miffed
at these Western superheroes who have come to occupy a place that he
once inhabited himself. At the same time, *Mickey 17*, like *Snowpiercer*
before it, is a class-inflected sci-fi drama that explores the most precarious figures within a power-laden enterprise, in this case nothing short of
interplanetary colonization. So, despite the implicit acknowledgment (and
thematization) of the hegemonic framework that bespeaks its material
conditions of production, the film encounters that framework from a position characterized by vulnerability and marginality. In Bong's earlier films,
such a position might be rooted in Korea's emergence out of Japanese
colonialism into US neoimperialism; in his later films, though rooted in
a genealogy that extends from a shabby Korean apartment complex, this
vulnerability becomes more generalizable.

In the interview that follows this essay, Bong Joon Ho speaks of
his abiding and obsessive desire to shoot water in his films, especially
in rain sequences, mentioning his admiration for the rainy car chase
scene in James Gray's *We Own the Night* (2007). Indeed, we can see

the prominence of water in its various states of matter throughout his oeuvre. In this respect, the falling snow outside the house at the end of *Parasite* might be regarded as a sublimated form of the earlier torrential rainstorm that flushed the Kims from the Parks' house and flooded their half-basement dwelling with sewage, the scent of which they could not remove from their clothing in time for the tragically fated garden party. With this film set in Seoul, all this water surely flows into the Han River, which serves as the birthplace and home for the monster in *The Host*. The falling snow from *Parasite* also recalls the apocalyptic, frozen land-scapes of *Snowpiercer*, with its invocation of the intransigent power of nature, and, more obliquely, the mud in *Memories of Murder* as a figure of entropy. The ice planet in *Mickey 17* offers an even larger canvas for such cinematic ambitions, thus resituating the dynamic interaction of mise-en-scène and mise en abyme away from a singular house and toward an interplanetary scale and relativity. But as becomes clearer as the scope becomes larger, to master water in its sundry forms, if only in cinema, is to regulate an element of nature that inherently refuses to be controlled. Thus, in Bong's films there is a disparity between the spectacular cinematic representation of water and the devastating effect it has on the landscapes and urbanscapes it flows into in large volumes, be it a deluge of rain or an avalanche of snow. We may think of this dis-parity as expressive in Bong's work not just of the vast power of natural forces but of social ones as well.

As the frame of attention in his films shifts from Korean and national to transnational and global terms (and then further still to interplanetary relations in *Mickey 17*), the stakes become greater, even as the means of addressing larger and larger problems fail to advance. We have gained ground in moving from a focus on incremental certainties (walnuts, toilet paper, bananas) to an interrogation of larger forms of kinship, and in proceeding from a preoccupation with makeshift families and flawed parents to an insight into global hegemons no longer compelled to maintain the customary air of benevolence, even as a facade. We have explored the various possibilities for escape, both fleeing outside of op-pressive systems and retreating inward for safe harbor. But as we have become more canny about our emergent geographies, we remain unsure about the subsequent course of action, about what is left to be done. To be sure, Bong Joon Ho's films are filled with clever characters who are forced to draw on limited resources and on whatever abilities they possess in order to rise to daunting challenges—to solve horrific crimes, to rescue children from monsters, to save beloved pets, to scheme for jobs to save a struggling family. These endeavors achieve varying degrees of success, but we cannot shake the strong sense of the building crisis that seems to underlie them. Ultimately, then, the most urgent task that Bong Joon Ho's films endeavor to undertake in the face of such crises is to see them as such. The most tangled of knots, it turns out, remain supremely difficult to untie.

Notes

1. The revised constitution was approved in October 1987. After elections in December 1987, Roh Tae-woo took office in February 1988.

2. Nam Lee reads *Barking Dogs Never Bite* as an expression of the moral anomie arising from compressed modernity (*Films* 92–94).

3. Elsewhere I have described this dynamic as *subsistence faming* (J. J. Jeon, *Vicious* 75–76).

4. Christina Klein reads the film as linking the surface crime (the murders in the film) to the deep crimes of the authoritarian state (882).

5. Nam Lee reads the photograph as connecting the detectives to the corruption of the Chun Doo-hwan regime (*Films* 76–77).

6. Shin Ji-hye details the persistent objections of prominent economist Ha-Joon Chang to low welfare investments by the South Korean government.

7. We catch a glimpse of US military operations in Iraq during a television news segment in the film.

8. The military engagements of the Korean War were brought to a halt with an armistice in 1953, but at the time of this writing, no formal resolution has been settled, though there has been some movement toward such a resolution in recent years.

9. Chung and Diffrient offer an insightful reading of this scene (175–76).

10. Meera Lee suggests that a focus of *The Host* is the "overlapping boundary between the monster and the human" (720).

11. Klein suggests that some of the most disturbing scenes in the film involve the deference of Korean characters to American interests, which become harmful to Koreans (889).

12. Michelle Cho offers a compelling account of the specific iconicity of Kim Hye-ja and Won Bin in Korean popular culture, particularly in relation to their faces ("Face").

13. For example, a *Koreaboo* article on Won Bin's wealth—titled "Koreans Discovered How Much Won Bin Makes from CFs and It Blew Their Minds"— follows its headline with the punchy comment, "No wonder he doesn't work."

14. Nikki Ji Yeon Lee discusses how *The Host* participates in a larger effort in the Korean film industry to integrate local content into a global market.

15. Jieun Kiaer and Loli Kim discuss the challenges that inhere in subtitling Korean in relation to *Parasite*.

16. Seung-hoon Jeong writes: "The extreme imagination of catastrophe thus betrays the impasses of the imagination, the incapacity for imagining a new, better society" (495).

17. I discuss *Okja* in relationship the the Trans-Pacific Partnership elsewhere (see J. J. Jeon, *Vicious* 177–84).

18. Kristen Angierski offers a reading of the film attentive to the ecological impact of global agribusiness.

19. Chungmoo Choi offers a comparative reading of the endings of *The Host* and *Snowpiercer* (162–63).

20. Gladys Lechini traces the role of the Washington Consensus in the politics of globalization, describing the Washington Consensus as "an international hegemonic structure—led by global dominant economic and political forces," which was able to gain control over "the policy-making and the domestic agenda of supposedly sovereign states, determining new forms of subordination and control. This asymmetrical network of social, political and cultural relations has prevented the countries of the periphery from implementing sovereign decisions in crucial areas of governance, with the consequent erosion of their democratic legitimacy" (10).

21. Annie McClanahan offers a usefully skeptical account of the utility of *neoliberalism* as a periodizing term.

22. I have in mind Giovanni Arrighi's definition of hegemony as the ability to provide the "motor force of a general expansion" (31).

23. E. San Juan Jr. writes: "With enforced 'free trade' in a global 'free market,' the US corporate elite would not be challenged anymore by new Koreas or Taiwans—the Washington Consensus would prevail as the new *Pax Americana*, the goal of the Project for a New American Century."

24. Joseba Gabilondo offers a skeptical reading of class relations in *Parasite*, writing: "a film that supposedly allows us to see 'real class conflict' becomes the one that actually restores a capitalist neoliberal order at a very global level (hence the unprecedented Oscar to a film in a language other than English). *Parasite* enacts a fantasy that keeps us from facing class conflict on a global level" (17).

25. As Stephen Neale has usefully argued, film genres are not rigid ahistorical categories but rather "processes of systemization" (51). My intent here is thus less to construct a taxonomy and more to highlight the generic elements that *Parasite* cites and puts into motion in its own generic play. Furthermore, my use of film genres throughout this essay is in this spirit.

26. Michael Szalay locates such dynamics generically in what he terms the "industrious family drama."

27. Marc Yamada offers a historical overview of the period in relation to cultural production (3–22).

28. Patrick Jagoda offers a useful account of gamification, writing: "Gamification . . . marks a condition of seepage or doubling through which game mechanics and activities influence work, leisure, thought, and social relations—key ways people interface with reality today. The games that inundate the present are action-oriented mediations that shape everyday experience through neoliberal principles" (12).

29. Video games seem to be the medium in which the battle royal genre obtains its purest form. Se-young Kim examines how the genre in video games (in relation to filmic antecedents) articulates contemporary anxieties about youth unemployment in East Asia.

30. In an interview, Bong likened the tepee to a Che Guevara T-shirt: "The context and meaning behind these actual things only exists as a surface-level thing" (Holub).

31. Hsuan Hsu offers a compelling account of the relationship between smell and social inequality (*Scent* 13–15).

An Interview with Bong Joon Ho |

This interview took place on January 25, 2021, via an online meeting platform. I spoke in English from my home in California, and Bong Joon Ho spoke in Korean from his office in Seoul. Unlike the final exchange between Curtis and Minsoo in *Snowpiercer*, we could understand each other when we spoke, but for the purposes of this publication, I decided to bring in a professional. So, in addition to Director Bong and myself, Sharon Choi was also present to provide translation services. Readers may remember Ms. Choi as Bong's translator during *Parasite*'s promotional and award season run in 2019–20, culminating in the film's historic success at the 2020 Academy Awards, where the film was the first non-English-language film to win Best Picture. I would like to express my deep gratitude for and my utter amazement with the thoroughness of Ms. Choi's translation. As I was transcribing the interview, I marveled at Ms. Choi's incredible phrase-by-phrase accuracy, nuance, and precision in her live translation.

Before the interview began, Director Bong revealed that he had been writing intensely over the past several days, so intensely in fact that he had injured himself somehow and was experiencing some pain. Nevertheless, he was incredibly generous with his time. I decided to refrain from noting all the laughter or other emotive moments by Director Bong throughout the interview, but I want to emphasize how spirited, kind, and engaging he was throughout the entire interview, with the small exception of his answer to the last question, where he modestly deflected when I asked him to reflect on his legacy. The following has been minimally edited, and only for the sake of clarity.

JOSEPH JONGHYUN JEON (JJJ): I want to begin with some questions about your childhood and early education before moving on to film. You were born in Daegu and then moved to Seoul during elementary school, to the Jamsil neighborhood. And this was a very historic moment. Of course, Jamsil was being developed in the decade or so before the Seoul Olympics. My father, who is much older than you are, is from a town not too far away from Daegu, and he moved to Seoul as a young boy. I kind of always think of my father as kind of a country boy at heart. I'm curious about your memories of Daegu and of your childhood. And what was it like to move from this provincial location to the big city?

BONG JOON HO (BJH): When I think of Daegu, I just remember it being really hot. I didn't have a lot of opportunities to go out and run around and play with other kids because as a boy, I was quite fragile. I had some kidney issues. So, I spent a lot of time at home. What I remember most is my father's study. He was in the arts. He did industrial design and graphic design. At the time my father taught at a university in Daegu, and that's why we lived there. And as he changed jobs, our entire family moved to Seoul. My father started working at a government institution, a design center. This was in the seventies and eighties, when the military dictatorship was at its peak. This is something that we can't comprehend now, but at the time it was a professional design center operated by the government, and the head of the center was actually a soldier. A military soldier. So, my father was really stressed out because this person knew nothing about design, but he was in charge of managing the center. My father had to communicate with him despite the fact that he knew nothing about design. What I remember is him coming back home after work and just being really stressed out. No one in our family was particularly political. We were just people who love art. But seeing how stressed he was, I think that allowed me to develop this aversion to the military dictatorship of the time. And that's what I remember most about first moving to Seoul. In Jamsil, we lived in an old apartment near the Han River. I would go there with my friends to hang around the river. And of course, you know, I would later shoot a film there [*The Host*], though I never knew at the time that that would happen.

JJJ: In a few of your movies, *Memories of Murder*, *Mother*, and *Okja*, for example, a lot of the energy of the story comes from the difference between rural and urban settings. Does this in part come from your childhood experience of moving from Daegu to Seoul? I realize that Daegu is also a city but a very different one, particularly in those days.

BJH: Daegu was probably the third- or fourth-largest city in Korea, but we lived on the edge of the city. So, it kind of felt like the countryside. We lived in front of a very large mountain, and it kind of felt suburban. It was on the edge of the city. There weren't that many people around. And then, you know, when we moved to Seoul, we started living in this huge apartment complex. And so similarly in *Okja*, you see Mija go from the countryside to these large metropolitan areas like Seoul and New York. For me, the change wasn't that extreme, but I think that is where those stories come from. I really missed Daegu for the first couple of years I started living in Seoul. I started getting really nostalgic. More than anything, we had to leave our dog in Daegu. We were unable to bring the dog to Seoul because at the time these apartment complexes had a rule where you couldn't have pets. It seems ridiculous now. Everyone owns pets in apartments, but at the time there were these strange regulations where you had to have a backyard or a garden to raise a dog. I really loved that dog, and we just had to leave him with some cousins in Daegu. That was the saddest part of all of this. I think that's why in *Okja* and *Barking Dogs Never Bite*, you see stories about pets.

JJJ: You went to Yonsei University, where you studied sociology. Why sociology?

BJH: I knew that I wanted to become a film director since I was in middle school, but I just couldn't get myself to apply to film school first because the competition was so fierce. The chances were like fifty to one, a hundred to one. Also, you had to take these practical exams where you had to act in front of the professors, like an audition, because in Korean film schools, it's both theater and film. I just didn't have it in me to do that. At the time, I really admired two Korean directors. They were the star directors of the eighties. Lee Jang-ho and Bae Chang-ho. When people talk about eighties Korean cinema, these two directors are always mentioned, and they were my heroes. I realized that neither of them went to film school. Bae Chang-ho studied business at Yonsei University. So, I realized that to become a film director, I should just study the humanities as an undergrad and instead join a cinema club as my extracurricular activity. I also thought that maybe after undergrad I could go to film school to get an MFA. And so, I was considering literature, sociology, media, just anything related to the humanities and media. I applied, and it just happened to be sociology. Even to this day, I feel like I don't know that much about sociology.

JJJ: That's funny because I feel like your movies are often sociological. They seem to be about groups of people and how groups of people interact.

BJH: There is definitely that aspect to my films, but I don't think I got it from studying books or taking sociology classes. I think it's thanks to the friends that I met studying this major. I still meet them to this day. It's about ten to fifteen friends. I shared a lot of conversations with them, communicated with them, and was able to really share the various diverse perspectives and interpretations they had about society. That's what really stayed with me. We would study together and have conversations together. So, rather than the curriculum of the school or the books that I had to study, it was really thanks to these conversations with my friends that my films ended up having that social aspect to them. Also, you know, I'm someone who lived through the 1980s, the 1980s to the 2000s, in Korea. Korea went through so many changes throughout those years, from the military dictatorship to the IMF crisis to the 2000s. I lived through that myself. So, rather than coming from some sort of academic field, a lot of it comes from my personal experience, like how I mentioned my father and how stressed he was about having a soldier as his boss at a design center. You know, that's a very personal episode that I had, but at the same time, it's also a portrait of the military dictatorship. I think those two are inseparable.

JJJ: I've read a lot of interviews where you talk about how when you were a child, you watched movies on television. We're about the same age. I was born in 1971. I think of myself as part of the TV generation. I watched a lot of television when I was growing up. In your films, TV is often featured, or it is there in the background. In *Memories of Murder*, for example, the detectives stop the interrogation to watch the television show *Inspector Chief* together. You also feature the TV news, and there are all sorts of other examples. Could you talk about how television influenced your filmmaking?

BJH: I don't really remember when I started loving movies. My oldest memories are from when I was five or six, and already at the time I really loved watching movies. Perhaps because I had to spend so much time at home. At the time I didn't have any choice but to watch what the TV channels were playing, because in Korea we only started getting VHS after the 1988 Seoul Olympics. Before then, we didn't have any choice but to watch movies that were playing on TV. Also, my mother hated the cinema. She would always say that it's full of germs because it never gets any sunlight throughout the year. So, our family didn't really go to movie theaters. I would go to the cinema by myself, and I remember going to the theaters by myself to watch films. But overwhelmingly I watched more movies on TV. There wasn't cable like there is today. There were only four to five channels: MBC, KBS, EBS, and, of course, AFKN [Armed Forces Korea Network]. I've mentioned this in several interviews, but on AFKN, I watched films by John Carpenter, Brian De Palma, and all these American, quite violent, R-rated films. A lot of strange B movies as well. On EBS, which is the educational channel, they played a lot of films by European auteurs like Fellini, Truffaut, Antonioni, and they would always play them on Sunday at noon or one o'clock. I remember constantly checking the newspaper for the TV schedule, checking which films I wanted to see.

JJJ: Finally on the issue of television, I know that there is a successful TV remake of *Snowpiercer* that we can watch here in the United States. And I've heard that there is a version of *Parasite* being adapted for television. What is your level of involvement in these ventures, and what you think about them?

BJH: With *Snowpiercer*, I was the executive producer. During the early stages of development, I would talk with the showrunner about the basic storyline and the direction of the TV show, but that was sort of the extent of my involvement. With *Parasite*, as one of the producers, I'm more actively involved in this project. Adam McKay is the writer, and he already has the basic storyline and is currently working on the story for each episode. Adam McKay's team and my team, we are constantly sharing outlines, reviewing each other's ideas. So, I'm more actively involved. I think this will really show Adam McKay's sense of satire and comedy. I'm quite looking forward to it.

JJJ: I'm looking forward to it as well. I recently saw your conversation with Director Lee Isaac Chung about his film *Minari*. You said something in that conversation that resonated with me. You were talking about the fire scene in the movie and how the film is concerned with water and fire. You said that directors are always preoccupied with capturing water. And then you said, I'm going to quote you here, "to me that is cinema. Before characters and events, those cinematic elements matter." And I don't want you to feel strange because I'm about to compare you to God, but this reminded me of the creation story in Genesis. Let there be light, let there be the sky and the sea, the land, vegetation, et cetera. Eventually human beings. I guess for me, your statement to Lee Isaac encapsulated something I find compelling in your films. They're not just stories about people, but they really build worlds. Could just talk a little bit about that statement, about the cinematic elements and why you think they're so important?

BJH: Yes, we spoke about fire and rain, with Lee Isaac Chung. I once had this obsession with shooting a really great rain scene. You see those sequences in films like *Seven Samurai* by Kurosawa Akira. And recently there was a great film by James Gray, *We Own the Night*. And there's an amazing car chase sequence that happens in the rain. So good. With *Memories of Murder* and *Mother*, you also have these important rain sequences. Rain ultimately is water. In *Mother* during the climax sequence, you see the character burn up the warehouse. With *Snowpiercer* and *Okja*, I wasn't able to shoot any rain sequences. So, I think my desire to shoot in the rain just exploded with *Parasite*, where you have that long rain sequence and the entire house being submerged under water. You can say that my obsession is still ongoing. With *Minari*, it's a small film, but it was really effective in how the film uses those elements. And I think this is something that only cinema can do, something that different mediums like theater or comics can't do. It concerns rain, water, fire, smoke, wind. You have the amazing sequence by John Ford, where you have the bride's veil blowing in the wind. In Tarkovsky's *The Sacrifice*, you have the entire house burning. Tarkovsky was such a master of water and fire. When I think about all the artists that I admire, the cinematic artists that I admire, they always handle water and fire, wind, and smoke. And I would really like to applaud Lee Isaac Chung for how he handled water and fire in *Minari*. As a producer, [I find that] water and fire are always tricky because of budget and time issues. You need to really prepare a lot, and it is not easy to handle. *Minari* was a low-budget film with a tight schedule. I know that they only had twenty-five shooting days. So, they were really effective in how they handled it. So, I'd just really like to send him a round of applause for it.

JJJ: You mention *Memories of Murder*. It reminded me of my favorite scene maybe from all your films, which is that opening long take at the first crime scene when Detective Park walks from the road. There's a footprint in the mud, and then he walks all the way to the corpse and then back again to the footprint. There's a tractor that comes by it and destroys the footprint. There's so much happening in that scene. There are people sliding down the embankment. It's kind of horrifying and funny at the same time. While you're speaking about water and elements, I was thinking about how mud is so important in that scene, not just because of the footprint but also the people sliding up and down the embankment. That scene is so effective because the viewer walks around in that world for as long as that take. Can you talk about that scene, why it was important, and how you made it?

BJH: So first, thank you for mentioning the part about the mud, because I want my films to feel very physical rather than conceptual. I want my films to seem tactile and very sensory. I want it to almost damage the viewers physically. And in that sense, the mud played a big role in that. That opening scene and that entire sequence in the opening of *Memories of Murder* presents to the audience that this is what this film is about. This is the atmosphere of the eighties because at the time, the crime scenes weren't managed very well. There was no order. It's not like the CIA or FBI crime scenes where you have CSI come in and you have the police line and everything is under control. Just literally it's a mud bath. In Korea, we often use the term *mud bath* casually to describe something that's a total mess. And that scene, you really literally see a mud bath in front of you. That scene was actually inspired by an interview I did with a local news reporter who worked on the case. He was the person who would be the first to run to the scene to report on the serial murder case that the film was about. The way he described it, he said as soon as he arrived, he just saw a bunch of footprints in the mud. It was a total mess. In his mind, it was like, are there ten murderers? What's going on? And later he realized that it was footprints from all the police officers. They were just stepping around, walking around, leaving their footprints behind. And he was flabbergasted. It was funny. It was horrific. And he just realized that nothing was under control. That's where I got the idea about the mud.

From the beginning I designed the scene as one long take. I wanted it to feel like I was live streaming how messy the crime scenes were in the eighties and have the audience participate in it, to have the audience actually be there and experience this massive situation. We prepared meticulously for that sequence because it involved very complicated blocking. We blocked everything from the direction the detective would come in, how they would slip, the direction of the tractor, and where the chief and the CSI members would be. We found the location early in prep. We were there all day to shoot that scene. We rehearsed in the morning. All the assistant directors were getting ready for it because we had more than one hundred extras. So, it was quite complicated. We spent the entire morning rehearsing. Then we had lunch and then spent the entire afternoon shooting. I think we shot about fourteen takes.

JJJ: Wow! Is that why in the *Mother* crime scene, they say, oh, the police all watch the TV show *CSI*? They know how to do this. You didn't want to go through all of that again?

BJH: Yes. In *Mother*, everything is under control. You have, you know, the CSI, the proper outfits coming and doing this and that with their little pincers.

JJJ: Getting back to the idea of mud baths in the 1980s, it's not just the police that are stuck in the mud. It's the entire era, Korea in the 1980s, the Chun Doo-hwan administration, the authoritarian government. When I watched *Memories of Murder*, I thought about

Peppermint Candy. I think you had the same cinematographer, Kim Hyeong-gu?

BJH: Yes, that's right.

JJJ: And I also thought of Fritz Lang's *M*, the great German expressionist film, which is also a film about the hysterical reaction to a serial killer. So, it's a story that is as much about the society affected by the murders as it is about the murders themselves. I wondered if you had those two films in mind in some way?

BJH: *Peppermint Candy* did have a lot of influence on *Memories of Murder*. Of course, we share the cinematographer, Kim Hyeong-gu, but also that film really shows the eighties and the military dictatorship. It does a great job of describing that era. And the main character, played by Sol Kyung-gu, he was once a detective as well, in charge of torturing the suspects. The way that that film describes the police station, the police force in general, really inspired *Memories of Murder*. Fritz Lang's *M* is such a masterpiece and a classic. But I think because it's such an old movie, I didn't really take it as a reference for *Memories of Murder*. What really helped me was actually two movies by Japanese directors, *Cure* by Kurosawa Kiyoshi and *Vengeance Is Mine* by Imamura Shōhei. In those two films, as with *M*, the serial killer is practically the protagonist. With *Memories of Murder*, as I previously mentioned, I interviewed a lot of people who were involved in the case, the local news reporter, the detectives, and residents of the neighborhood where the murders happened. I did a lot of research, but the only person that I wasn't able to meet was the serial killer, the actual murderer, because at the time, the case was unsolved. And so, I was so curious about the murderer. I really wanted to talk with him and understand his motivations. But because that was not possible, I watched films that dealt with murderers. *Cure* and *Vengeance Is Mine* were two films that did that. And though the serial killers in those two films are very different, they were very inspiring because with those films, I was able to see the face of the murderer.

During the process of screenwriting, I was influenced by two books. The first one is by an actual FBI agent. His name is John Douglas. He was the person who invented the profiling method and the first official profiler at the FBI. He wrote this book called *Mindhunter*, which was recently adapted by David Fincher for Netflix as a TV series. But the original book, *Mindhunter*, was a big influence because it contains a lot of interviews with actual serial killers. These killers were some of the most famous serial killers in America, like Ted Bundy. I read through those interviews and tried to figure out what those serial killers and the killer of the case in *Memories of Murder* shared, what qualities they shared. I read that book a lot while writing the script. The second book is a graphic novel called *From Hell* by Alan Moore, who also did *Watchmen*. This graphic novel was recommended to me by an acquaintance, and it deals with Jack the Ripper, who was a serial killer at Whitechapel, London, in the nineteenth century. He's the first official serial killer in modern history. The actual killer was never caught. There are just a lot of theories around it, but the person was never caught. I thought that the graphic novel did a great job of conveying the atmosphere of the Victorian era, the nineteenth century. It kind of made it seem as if the era was the killer. It was the era that was responsible for all those murders. That was a huge influence on *Memories of Murder*, because while writing the script I kept asking myself, why did we fail? Why did they never catch the killer? I decided to focus the answer on dealing with the limitations of the times, the darkness of the times of the eighties. It was a huge influence.

JJJ: I read that while you were doing research for the film, you became very absorbed in the crime, so much so that it was affecting you emotionally and exhausting you. That exhaustion and frustration seems reflected in the film and in the detectives who get increasingly frustrated and exhausted. There's that great scene where they both have their heads down on the desk and they're just saying, what are we going to do? And there's a wonderful—I think some people call these details in your films, Bong-tails? There's a little detail in that scene where there's a magazine open and you can see a picture of Lee Soon-ja, Chun Doo-hwan's wife. A perfect little detail. I'm curious, given how much emotional energy you put into the film, what was your reaction a few years ago when they finally discovered the identity of the real killer? [In 2019, DNA evidence and his confession confirmed that Lee Chun-jae, who was already in prison for another crime, was the real killer. He could not be prosecuted for the crime because the statute of limitations had expired.]

BJH: When I finally saw the photo of his face, I felt quite vexed because the film is essentially a journey of trying to find the face of the murderer. You have three suspects in the film. As you go over each suspect, it feels like you're getting closer to the actual murderer. With the third suspect, played by Park Hae-il, his face is portrayed as the killer's face that we all wanted to see. All the detectives and even people in the audience project their desire to check the face of the murderer on this actor's face. And of course, it could be quite dangerous as you never know for certain. But in the end as you know, they never find the killer. It seems 90 percent certain that the third suspect is the one. But unless you're 100 percent sure, it doesn't really matter. And so, the killer's face sort of disappears into the darkness of this long tunnel forever. On the day I actually saw the news piece about the killer, I think I spent that day just feeling very blank and absent-minded. It had been sixteen years since we completed the film. I talked to Song Kang-ho and the producers of the film about how we all saw the article. But thankfully, he was in prison since 1995. Usually serial killers, they can't stop the murders unless they die or they're in prison. But Lee Chun-jae, the murderer, he was already in prison for a different case, since 1995. The Hwaseong serial killings stopped in the early nineties, and that was why. It still gives me goose bumps thinking about how many more victims there could have been if he hadn't been in prison. So that's kind of just how I decided to think about it. It's a relief that he was in prison since 1995. I thought about going to visit him to talk to him, but I didn't do it.

JJJ: As I've been writing this book about your work, I've thought a lot about *Mother* in particular. In some ways, it stands out as a different film than your others. It's the darkest one of your films. It also comes before two English-language films with Western actors and an international sensibility. *Mother* in contrast seems the opposite of international. It seems very Korean. It begins when the Mercedes-Benz drives through the town, and that's the international element in the movie. It's set in a very Korean locale and has no Western actors. I'm curious about what you were thinking about when you made this movie. And if you have any thoughts about why you move toward these very different kinds of internationally oriented films directly following *Mother*.

BJH: I first have to explain my filmmaking pattern and process. I usually spend a very long time preparing and developing the idea, and the projects always overlap. With *Mother* and "Shaking Tokyo," which is an omnibus film that was shot in Japan, and *Snowpiercer*—these three films, I started preparing for them around 2004. So, I spent a long period for each project. When *Memories of Murder* was released in 2003—I mentioned earlier that I watched a lot of TV when I was young because I just stayed mostly at home—I noticed that Kim Hye-ja basically ruled over Korean television. She was the nation's mother. She was in a bunch of very famous TV shows. She's an iconic actress for playing all these mother roles. I started developing this obsession over wanting to show a different side of this actress. I wanted to show a very dark and hysterical side to her. So, I started the project in 2004, and at the time I had a very short treatment. I met with the actress to talk about it. At the same time, producers from Japan and France approached me about making a short film about Tokyo with Michel Gondry and Leos Carax. So that's why I did "Shaking Tokyo." Around the same time, also, I found the graphic novel for *Snowpiercer* at a bookstore in Korea. The moment I read it, I knew how difficult it would be to actually make this film. But I developed a strong desire to make a film about trains. Ever since I was little, I really loved trains and thought that trains were so cinematic because of the way they move and twist and turn. I was also a huge fan of this Japanese anime called *Galaxy Express 999*. Around 2004 and 2005, I had these three projects developing inside my brain at the same time. They all started from very personal impulses and desires to tell these stories. I never intended to control how I place my projects in my filmography, how this project will be international and then after that I'll do this local very Korean project. You know, I don't look at my projects in that way. I generally just follow what I'm obsessed with at the time. With *Parasite* as well, I never intended to come back to Korea to do a fully Korean film. I just thought of the idea around 2013 and thought it would make a great, fun film. So, I decided to start that project. In short, I never really manage my filmography. I just follow my impulses of the time, and that's how my project or my projects are placed. I can never control how it will all take shape.

JJJ: I appreciate how your projects always begin with a personal obsession, and so I sometimes wonder when I am watching one of your films where you personally are in your movie, how your personal ideas or obsessions manifest in the movie. In thinking about *Memories of Murder*, that scene of exhaustion seems to reflect your exhaustion with researching this brutal case. I read somewhere that *Barking Dogs Never*

Bite was filmed in either the building you were living in or some similar kind of building. In *Mother*, the place that I think about is the golf course scene, which I love. Do-joon and Jin-tae arrive. They damage the car, and they're all ready to fight. But then there's this considerable amount of time where they just wander around the golf course. Korean golf courses are so strange, and they seem full of wonder about the strangeness of the place. And there's a great line in which Do-joon has to remind himself that he is there for revenge. Almost like he forgot why he was there. I know you get a lot of questions about how you deal with genre. It's almost like he's trying to remind himself what genre the film is. Can you tell me a little bit about that scene and what you were trying to accomplish there? It was such a surprise when, after they break the mirror and they run in, they just kind of like wander as if they're taking a nice walk through the forest for a few minutes.

BJH: I have no experience with golf. I don't play golf. So, it was the first time I ever visited a golf course. I was amazed too. Wow, this is cool. There were so many stars, and it looked all so great. We were introduced to that golf course by our head producer because usually golf courses don't like lending their location for filming. It's really difficult to get permission. But thankfully, the head of the production company, he has a lot of famous and wealthy acquaintances and knows owners of these golf courses, so he let us shoot there. I was actually feeling the same things that Do-joon was feeling there. They go around the pond. He picks up the golf balls in the pond. We heard that there are a bunch of golf balls, usually in the water. They go from this very shabby place and the downtown of a country town where you have the mother cutting up ingredients for the herbal medicine. They start from this very shabby place and take a taxi to this different world. So, the golf course scene sort of shows how they're accessing a different world. And I think overall, with *Mother*, you have a lot of these disparate things coming together and sort of getting jumbled up together. The locations, they feel urban. They also feel like they're in the countryside. With Won Bin's character, on one hand, he seems very childlike and innocent, but you also sense this darkness that he's hiding. I think that sense of duality begins at the golf course scene.

JJJ: There's another scene from *Mother* that has a small detail that I love. And it leads me to a question I have about money in your films.

This is the scene where the mother takes the umbrella off the poor man's cart. She tries to pay him, holding out two bills, but he only takes one of them. I realized that this is a repeated trope in your movies. There's the scene in *The Host* where Nam-il tries to pay the homeless man for his empty soju bottles, and the homeless man hits him with a soju bottle because he starts to take them without asking. And then there's the scene in *Parasite* where Mrs. Park is paying Ki-woo. She counts out the bills, puts them in an envelope, but then takes a few out first before she gives the envelope to Ki-woo. These scenes all strike me as similar in that they are all transactions, but they're a little bit different from a usual financial transaction. I was curious to know what your attitude toward money is and what you are trying to say or show in those scenes.

BJH: Thank you for pointing out that detail. Even in *The Host*, you have that scene where someone's counting the bills that are soaked in water and then that creature comes to hit him. It's always quite fun shooting money because essentially, my films, a lot of them deal with capitalism. They are stories about money, and inevitably money is something that controls all of us. We don't want to be under money's control, but it's almost inevitable. And so when I see shots of bills, you know, close-up shots of bills, when I see them on the monitor, I feel quite strange. I don't think my films go as deep into analyzing money as Robert Bresson's *Money* does. But I think when you see characters handle money, and you see their attitudes toward money, you end up learning a lot about who they are as people. Especially when you see them handling cash and you see how they're handling cash, it's really effective in describing what kind of people these characters are. A detail that I really like in *Mother* is when Jin-tae assesses the thickness of the stack of bills that he receives from the mother. Because you see in the film, he gets money from her a couple of times. In the amusement park, when she hands him the envelope with the stack of bills inside, he doesn't even bother to count the bills. Instead, he checks out how thick the stack is. I think that just explains everything about that character. And at the end of the film, when Do-joon is released from prison, he buys a used Mercedes with that money. So, you have a Mercedes in the beginning and then at the end of the film. But I thought that the way that Jin-tae measured the thickness of the stack explained the essence of who that character is. On the other hand, you have that old man taking only one of two bills that the mother gives to him, and that represents his sense of self-worth and his attitude toward money. I think that this helps the audience really trust the decisive testimony that he gives at the end about what actually happened with the murder. It helps the audience believe in him. So, the way he handles money early on in the film gives credibility to what he says about witnessing the murder later on.

JJJ: You remind me that money in *The Host* is always comic. There's the scene where the family tries to bribe the official with a bag of coins. And there's another scene where the grandfather negotiates to get all that equipment from the gangsters, and the gangster tells him that they take credit cards. It's a funny transaction. This leads me to a question about comedy because *The Host* in particular is so tragic but also really funny. The scene that jumps to mind here is, of course, the mourning scene, where the family is in that public mourning center. It's very somber. They think that Hyun-seo, this young girl, has died. They start crying and it's really sad. And then they keep crying, and it becomes funny and absurd. There's that woman who is told that she must move her car because it's illegally parked. And then the guy in the hazmat suit walks in and poses in that absurd stance. And it's all very funny. One of the things I love about your films is that humor. It reminds me of old physical comedy, like that of Charlie Chaplin or Buster Keaton, that requires no dialogue. Can you talk about how you incorporate those elements into your films?

BJH: With those comedy, slapstick elements, I'm not exactly trying to emulate Buster Keaton or Chaplin, though in *The Host*, you see slapstick. There is that part where the agent in the hazmat suit slips. For me, these comedy elements are just a part of reality. When you have tragedy and comedy happening at the same time, it feels very confusing and very chaotic. But I think that really captures the specifically Korean sense of chaos. Things like that happen around me all the time. You have something very serious happening, but at the same time, it's funny. I think in order for people to feel like one sort of emotion, you need to have the situation organized in your head and form a narrative on it. You have to have all the conditions clearly laid out and understand them. But when something happens, when an event unfolds, usually it's very messy and very chaotic, and you don't have the leisure to feel one singular emotion. So, for me, it's not like I'm trying to insert comedic or slapstick elements into my films per se. I'm just trying to capture what is realistic to me and specifically what is realistic in Korea. Because when you go to funerals, you will have people come up to you and ask you to move your car.

JJJ: I have a question about *Parasite*. It's a Korean class drama of course. And you've mentioned in interviews being inspired by Kim Ki-young. But it strikes me that one important difference from modern Korean class dramas on film and television is that Nathan Park isn't the typical evil *chaebol* figure. And he's a very specific sort of technology entrepreneur. He makes maps. Specifically virtual technology maps. And I was just thinking about all the maps in your films, like the maps of the tracks in *Snowpiercer* that go around the world. The map of the crime scenes in *Memories of Murder*, the map of the sewer systems in *The Host*. Lucy Mirando has a map locating all the miracle pigs around the world in her presentation at the beginning of *Okja*. And in *Parasite*, there's a moment where Ki-taek is driving and says, I don't need a GPS anywhere south of the thirty-ninth parallel. I'm curious why you made Nathan Park a mapmaker.

BJH: I don't really have a big particular reason other than I enjoy looking at maps. I like looking at Naver Maps, Google Maps, Google Earth. I think I have a desire to look at everything from a bird's-eye point of view. I'm not a control freak. I'm not that sort of person, but I do get a sense of excitement when I'm able to just look at everything all at once. I did this dumb thing when I was writing the scenario for *Snowpiercer* where I spread out all the pages of the script on the floor so that I could have a bird's-eye view of the entire script. It was kind of silly because when you look at it from afar, you can't really read what's on the script. But I just had a desire to look at it all just in one view, and maybe I think that I'm able to control it when I do that. I also tend to spread out all the storyboards that I drew so that I can also just look at it from like a bird's-eye perspective.

JJJ: Speaking of *Snowpiercer*, I read an interview where you stated that it was the last thirty-five-millimeter film shot in Korea. Because when you returned to Korea from shooting the picture—am I getting this right?—you discovered that the labs couldn't process that format anymore. So, I'm curious if there's any connection between the fact that this is the last thirty-five-millimeter film in Korea and the fact that the film is about the last surviving members of the human species. The train's engine room feels very much like a film projector to me. I noticed that the Wilford logo looks a little bit like the logo for the Weinstein Company. And Ed Harris in the movie, in many ways, his role is very similar to his role in *The Truman Show*, which is this TV producer as a god. So, I was wondering if there was any kind of connection there, even subconsciously, between the film's plot and the Korean film industry. Is there a connection between the Korean film industry and the human apocalypse?

BJH: I had no idea that film would go extinct so quickly. Because when I released *Mother* in 2009, we handed film prints to all the movie theaters and people were still shooting in thirty-five-millimeter negatives. But during those two or three years in the early 2010s, everyone started shooting in digital, and the industry changed so fast. All the processing labs shut down. With *Snowpiercer*, we shot it at the Barrandov Studios in the Czech Republic. So, we processed the film in the Czech Republic and then we brought it all back to Korea. But when I came back, we found out that all the labs were shut down, and all the film prints are being held at the Korean Film Archive. It's almost like film has become this artifact of a bygone era. It happened so fast that it wasn't something that I was able to predict. So, there aren't any symbols or metaphors of it in the film itself, but we did witness the extinction of film, and the actual movie is about the extinction of the human race.

With Ed Harris in his roles, like in *The Truman Show*, he has the ability to convey the sense of a master manipulator, the all-controlling person, because he's so charismatic. And that's why I thought he was perfect for the role of Wilford. With the Weinstein Company, when we were shooting and designing the film, they had nothing to do with that. They acquired the film when we were working on postproduction. So, during the financing and production stage, the company had nothing to do with the project. They acquired it at the Asian film market when it was almost completed. And coincidentally that W does seem quite similar. I think when you make films, these coincidences often happen.

JJJ: Yes, I figured. I wasn't looking for any conspiracy theory. I have a question about your screenwriting, and this is where we began because you write so vigorously that you've injured yourself. I noticed that when you talk about storytelling in interviews, you often sound like a novelist.

You talk about perspective and point of view, and deliberate and careful plotting. You seem to take great care as a writer. I know you write your own screenplays, and have written the screenplays for, I believe, *Motel Cactus* [*Motel seoninjang*, 1997] and *Sea Fog* [*Haemoo*, 2014] as well. A few others. Could you talk a little bit about your approach just as a writer, and specifically that aspect of your filmmaking?

BJH: There are a couple films by other directors that I wrote the screenplays for, like *Sea Fog* and *Antarctic Journal* [*Namgŭkilgi*, 2005]. With *Motel Cactus*, I was also the assistant director, but I wasn't the lead writer for those projects. I took more of an assisting role. But with my own films, I am the lead writer. I would say I write about 80 to 90 percent of all my scripts, and usually my cowriters take on an assisting role, where they handle a lot of the research. Just in terms of time, I spend more time as a writer than as a director. I spend more days writing. And so, sometimes I feel like my main job is not a film director, but actually a writer. Screenwriting, it's a lonely process. I'm actually having a hard time these days because all the coffee shops in Korea are shut down right now.[1] Usually I like to move around to three coffee shops a day to write. That's the habit that I developed as a writer in the past few decades. But now that I'm just writing at home and in my office, my productivity isn't that great. I'm progressing quite slowly.

JJJ: I realize that this next question could be potentially sensitive, but I did want to at least ask about your maternal grandfather, Park Tae-won, who is a famous and somewhat controversial novelist. I guess the question would just be if you ever think about that legacy? And if you don't want to answer that question, I completely understand.

BJH: It's not a sensitive question at all because his story is now well known in Korea. If we were in the early eighties, it would have been censored because he went to North Korea, but now his books are freely published. There was a theater piece about him. If you read his books, his works, they feel very modernistic. He did a lot of formal experiments. One famous Korean literary critic compared him to James Joyce, the author of *Dubliners*. When I was little during the military dictatorship, my family didn't really like to talk about him. He was kind of a taboo topic within our family. They were very careful in talking about how he went to North Korea during the Korean War, but a lot of families were separated at the time. So, it's not something too uncommon. I just heard that my mother's father, my maternal grandfather, was a novelist. And that his novels could not be published in South Korea. And that in itself formed this sense of mystery around him. I heard that you could find his books in university libraries and in old used bookstores. So, at the time I didn't even enjoy reading novels, but I would go to the used bookstores to look for what novels were there.

JJJ: What do you think the next part of your career will look like? What are the projects you're looking forward to working on? How has the success of *Parasite* changed things for you, opened up doors?

BJH: I've mentioned this in previous interviews, but currently I'm working on one Korean project and one American project. With both projects, I started working on them much before *Parasite*. So, nothing has really changed. The American project is based on a true story. But with that one, there were a couple changes. So, that project is being delayed. Instead, I'm working on another American project. So as always, I'm working on a Korean and American project at the same time. I'm writing the scripts and working on the artwork for it as well. But the Korean project, I started working on it much before *Parasite*. With regard to everything that happened with *Parasite*, to me they just feel like fun events that happened. We didn't make the film to go to Cannes or receive awards at the Academy. The film was already made before all of that happened. It's not as if anyone makes films for those purposes. And even if you do, nothing really works out as planned. So now everything that happened with *Parasite* are just memories that I cherish. I'm just doing what I've always done and continuing to work on my projects.

JJJ: Last question, and I think just listening to your answers to previous questions, I think you're going to really hate this question, but I'm going to ask it anyway. So, imagine somebody picking up this book with this interview in a hundred years from a dusty library shelf. What would you like that person to know about you and what would you like them to know about your work?

BJH: Just that Joseph Jeon is an amazing professor.

JJJ: I'm not sure I could print that.

BJH: In the past year Sharon and I have had so many conversations and interviews about *Parasite* and my previous films. But the questions that you asked today, they felt very new and fresh and so detailed. So, I really enjoyed this conversation, and that's what I meant.

Figure 21. Bong Joon Ho with translator Sharon Choi (*left side*) and Joseph Jeon after the interview, which was conducted online.

JJJ: I tried to choose questions that I thought might interest you because I watched every single one of those interviews preparing for this. And I felt like I couldn't ask you those same questions. I didn't want you to get bored. But thank you so much. I'm so grateful for your time and generosity.

BJH: When are you getting vaccinated?

JJJ: I don't know. I mean, people are attacking the Capitol,[2] so lots of problems here. They say right now that people that are not high priority will maybe get it in the summer. I usually come to Seoul every summer, so I hope I can get it before I come, but I don't know.

BJH: I think things will get better soon. I should be able to get to Los Angeles soon. It would be nice to have a cup of coffee.

JJJ: I would like that very much. Do you mind if I just take a very quick picture of us? I'm just going to do a screenshot here (figure 21). Okay. Great. Thank you so much! I'm really, really grateful! Have a wonderful day.

Notes

1. This interview took place in 2021 during the COVID-19 pandemic, when many businesses like coffee shops had to shut down in South Korea.

2. A few weeks before this interview, protestors contesting the results of the 2020 US presidential elections stormed the Capitol building in Washington, DC.

1994
Paeksaekin (White Man)
Republic of Korea
Executive producer: Lee Byung-hoon
Producer: Jegal Yong
Director: Bong Joon Ho
Screenplay: Lee Byung-hoon, Bong Joon Ho
Editors: Bong Joon Ho, Kim Suk-woo, Chae Hui-byung, Lee Kyung-won
Cinematography: Yoo Seung-ho, Kim Han-kyung, Lee Dae-hui, Lee Ha-rim
Principal cast: Kim Roi-ha (protagonist, white-collar worker), Ah Nae-sang (No
Dong-ja), Kim Sang-won (office worker), Kim Dae-yeop (office worker), Lee
Sang-yeop (voice)
Format: 16 mm, color
18 minutes
Description: Bong made this film before entering film school. White-collar
worker finds a severed finger on his way to work, and it becomes the object
of his fascination throughout the day.

1994
P'ŭreim sogŭi kiŏktŭl (Memories in My Frame)
Republic of Korea
Director: Bong Joon Ho
Screenplay: Bong Joon Ho
Cinematography: Lee Sugil, Lee Hyun-jin
Music: Song Byeong-joon
Art direction: Cho Young-sam
Principal cast: Ch'oe Sŏngu (boy)
Format: 16 mm, color
5 minutes
Description: Student film made at the Korean Academy of Film Arts. Vignette
about a young boy who looks for his lost dog.

1994
Chilimyŏllyŏl (Incoherence)
Republic of Korea
Production: Korean Academy of Film Arts
Director: Bong Joon Ho
Screenplay: Bong Joon Ho
Editors: Bong Joon Ho, Jeong Seon-yeong
Cinematography: Cho Yongkyu, Son Tae-ung
Music: An Hye-suk
Art direction: Cho Young-sam
Principal cast: Yu Yeon-su (professor), Lim Sang-hyo (Manager Kim), Yoon Il-ju (editorial writer), Sin Dong-hwan (newspaper boy), Bong Joon Ho (newspaper boy's brother), Kim Sun-hwa (violent woman), Kim Ro-ha (prosecutor), Im Jae Hong (student)
Format: 16 mm, color
31 minutes
Description: Student film made at the Korean Academy of Film Arts for Bong's thesis. A series of satirical vignettes about the hypocrisy of prominent men in Korean society, including a university professor, newspaper editorial writer, and prosecutor.

2000
P'ŭllandasŭŭi kae (Barking Dogs Never Bite)
Republic of Korea
Production: Uno Film
Executive producer: Cha Seung-jae
Producer: Jo Min-whan
Distribution: Cinema Service
Director: Bong Joon Ho
Original story: Bong Joon Ho
Screenplay: Bong Joon Ho, Son Tae-ung, Song Ji-ho
Editor: Lee Eun-su
Cinematography: Cho Yong-kyu
Music: Jo Seong-woo
Art direction: Lee Young
Principal cast: Lee Sung-jae (Yun-ju), Bae Doona (Hyun-nam), Kim Ho-jung (Eun-sil), Byun Hee-bong (janitor), Ko Soo-hee (Jang-mi)
Format: 35 mm, color
106 minutes
Description: Bong's debut feature film. A dramatic comedy set in an apartment complex in Seoul, the film focuses on a humanities graduate student who struggles to obtain a full-time position at a university and on the social life at the apartment complex where he spends much of his time.

2003
Sarinŭi Ch'uŏk (*Memories of Murder*)
Republic of Korea
Production: Sidus
Executive producers: Cha Seung-jae, No Jong-yun
Producer: Kim Mu-ryeong
Distribution: CJ Entertainment
Director: Bong Joon Ho
Screenplay: Bong Joon Ho, Shim Sung-bo
Editor: Kim Sun-min
Cinematography: Kim Hyung-koo
Music: Taro Iwashiro
Production design: Ryu Seong-hui
Principal cast: Song Kang-ho (Detective Park), Kim Sang-kyung (Detective Seo),
    Kim Roi-ha (Detective Cho), Song Jae-ho (Sergeant Shin), Byun Hee-bong
    (Sergeant Koo), Park Hae-il (Park Hyeon-gyu), Park No-shik (Kwang-ho)
Format: 35 mm, color
131 minutes
Description: A dramatic thriller depicting the Hwaseong serial murders, which
    occurred in Korea between 1986 and 1994 and remained unsolved until
    2019. In a rural Korean town, two detectives with very different investigative
    methods partner to find the killer.

2004
Inp'ŭlluenja (*Influenza*)
Republic of Korea
Producer: Joh Neung-yeon
Director: Bong Joon Ho
Editor: Lee Moon-ho
Cinematography: Kim Byung-jung
Music: An Hye-sook
Principal cast: Yoon Je-moon (unemployed man), Ko Soo-hee (man's accomplice)
Format: video, black and white, color
28 minutes
Description: A mockumentary about an unemployed man who, with an ac-
    complice, is caught committing a series of crimes on various CCTV cameras
    around Seoul.

2004
"Shingk'ŭ & raijŭ" (Sink & Rise)
Republic of Korea
Director: Bong Joon Ho
Cinematography: Je Chang-gyu

Art direction: Park Sang-hun
Principal cast: Byun Hee-bong (food stand owner), Yoon Je-moon (father), Jeong In-sun (daughter)
6 minutes
Description: Part of a collection of short films by Korean Academy of Film Arts students, titled *Tijit'ŏl tanp'yŏn omnibŏsŭ p'ŭrojekt'ŭ igong* (*Digital Short Film Omnibus Twentidentity*). Buying a snack for his daughter, a man gets into an argument about whether boiled eggs will float in water.

2006
Koemul (*The Host*)
Republic of Korea
Production: Ch'ŏngŏram Films
Executive producers: Choe Yong-bae, Kim U-taek
Distribution: Showbox Entertainment
Director: Bong Joon Ho
Screenplay: Bong Joon Ho, Ha Joon-won, Baek Cheol-hyeon
Editor: Kim Sun-min
Cinematography: Kim Hyung-koo
Music: Lee Byung-woo
Production design: Ryu Seong-hui
Principal cast: Song Kang-ho (Gang-du), Byun Hee-bong (Hee-bong, Gang-du's father), Park Hae-il (Nam-il), Bae Doona (Nam-joo), Ko A-sung (Hyun-seo)
Format: 35 mm, color
119 minutes
Description: Monster movie about a terrifying creature that results from a US military decision to dump chemicals into the Han River in Seoul. The plot centers on a family whose child is abducted by the monster and their attempt to get her back.

2008
"Shaking Tokyo"
Japan
Production: Comme des Cinémas
Producer: Sadai Yuji
Distribution: Liberation Entertainment
Director: Bong Joon Ho
Screenplay: Bong Joon Ho
Cinematography: Fukumoto Jun
Music: Lee Byung Woo
Production design: Harada Mitsuo
Principal cast: Kagawa Teruyuki (the man), Aoi Yu (pizza delivery girl), Takenaka Naoto (pizzeria owner)

Format: 35 mm, color

30 minutes

Description: Final segment of the omnibus film *Tokyo!*, which was made with two other directors (Michel Gondry and Leos Carax). Bong's short is a about a *hikikomori* (or shut-in) who ventures finally out of his home to find the pizza delivery girl with whom he has fallen in love.

2009

Madǒ (Mother)

Republic of Korea

Production: Barunson

Executive producers: Mun Yangkwon

Producers: Seo Woo-sik, Park Tae-joon

Distribution: CJ Entertainment

Director: Bong Joon Ho

Story: Bong Joon Ho

Screenplay: Park Eun-gyo, Bong Joon Ho

Editor: Mun Se-gyeoung

Cinematography: Hong Kyung-pyo

Music: Lee Byung-woo

Production design: Ryu Seong-hui

Principal cast: Kim Hye-ja (mother), Won Bin (Do-joon), Jin Goo (Jin-tae), Yoon Je-moon (Je-moon, detective), Jun Mi-sun (Mi-sun), Moon Hee-ra (Ah-jung)

Format: 35 mm, color

128 minutes

Description: Dramatic thriller set in a small Korean town. Feeling that the local police have been mistaken, a doting mother conducts her own investigation of a murder for which her mentally disabled son is accused.

2011

"Iki" (Iki)

Japan

Director: Bong Joon Ho

3 minutes

Description: A short film about a girl who finds another girl lying down on the beach. Appeared in *3.11 A Sense of Home*, a project produced in honor of the victims of the March 3, 2011, Tohoku earthquake in Japan. The filmmakers involved in the project were asked to make films that would run for three minutes and eleven seconds.

2013

Sǒlgukyǒlch'a (Snowpiercer)

Republic of Korea

Production: Moho Films, Opus Pictures
Executive producers: Park Chan-wook, Lee Tae Hun
Producers: Park Tae Joon, Choi Dooho, Back Jisun, Robert Bernacchi
Distribution: CJ Entertainment, Weinstein Company
Director: Bong Joon Ho
Original story: Jacques Lob, Benjamin Legrand, Jean-Marc Rochette (*Le Transperceneige*)
Screenplay: Bong Joon Ho, Kelly Masterson
Editor: Steve M. Choe, Changju Kim
Cinematography: Hong Kyung-pyo
Music: Marco Beltrami
Production design: Ondřej Nekvasil
Principal cast: Chris Evans (Curtis), Song Kang-ho (Namgoong Minsoo), Ed Harris (Wilford), John Hurt (Gilliam), Tilda Swinton (Minister Mason), Jamie Bell (Edgar), Octavia Spencer (Tanya), Ko A-sung (Yona), Alison Pill (teacher)
Format: 35 mm, color
126 minutes
Description: Sci-fi action drama set in an apocalyptic future about a train carrying the last surviving human beings on earth. Poor passengers from the rear of the train revolt and move progressively forward toward the engine to take control.

2017
Okja (Okcha)
United States, Republic of Korea
Production: Plan B Entertainment, Lewis Pictures, Kate Street Picture Company
Executive producers: Pauline Fischer, Collin Creighton, Stan Wlodkowski, Kim Woosang, Brad Pitt, Sarah Esberg, Christina Oh
Producers: Tilda Swinton, Sandro Kopp, Ted Sarandos, Dede Gardner, Jeremy Kleiner, Lewis Taewan Kim, Dooho Choi, Woo Sik Seo, Bong Joon Ho
Distribution: Netflix, Next Entertainment World
Director: Bong Joon Ho
Story: Bong Joon Ho
Screenplay: Bong Joon Ho, Jon Ronson
Editor: Yang Jinmo
Cinematography: Darius Khondji
Music: Jaeil Jung
Production design: Kevin Thompson, Lee Ha Jun
Principal cast: Tilda Swinton (Lucy and Nancy Mirando), Ahn Seo-hyun (Mija), Paul Dano (Jay), Jake Gyllenhaal (Johnny Wilcox), Byun Hee-bong (Hee Bong, Mija's grandfather), Steven Yeun (K), Giancarlo Esposito (Frank Dawson), Choi Woo-shik (Kim Woo-shik)
Format: digital, color

120 minutes

Description: Comedic drama about a genetically engineered "super pig." The young Korean girl who raised her fights the giant multinational corporation that produced the pig and a group of ecoterrorists in order to bring her beloved pet home.

2019

Kisaengch'ung (Parasite)
Republic of Korea
Production: Barunson E&A, CJ Entertainment
Executive producers: Miky Lee, Heo Min-heoi
Producers: Bong Joon Ho, Kwak Sin Ae, Moon Yang Kwon, Jang Young Hwan
Distribution: CJ Entertainment
Director: Bong Joon Ho
Story: Bong Joon Ho
Screenplay: Bong Joon Ho, Han Jin Won
Editor: Yang Jinmo
Cinematography: Hong Kyung-pyo
Music: Jung Jae-il
Art direction: Lee Ha-jun
Principal cast: Song Kang-ho (Ki-taek), Lee Sun-kyun (Dong-ik), Cho Yeo-jeong (Yeon-gyo), Choi Woo-shik (Ki-woo), Park So-dam (Ki-jung), Lee Jung-eun (Moon-gwang), Jang Hye-jin (Chung-sook), Park Myung-hoon (Geun-sae)
Format: digital, color
132 minutes
Description: Black comedy about a poor family that cleverly connives its way into comfortable service jobs for a wealthy family in a beautiful modern home, deposing the existing housekeeper as part of its plan. The family members' enjoyment of their new life, however, is cut short when the former house-keeper returns and learns of their deceptions.

Other Credits

1994
2001 Imaejin (2001 Imagine)
Republic of Korea
Director: Jang Joon-hwan
Screenplay: Jang Joon-hwan
Editors: Bong Joon Ho, Jang Joon-hwan
Cinematography: Bong Joon Ho
Music: Park Kalin
Art direction: Cho Young-sam
Principal cast: Park Hee-soon, An Jin-hui, Kim Kyung-ran

Format: 16 mm, color
30 minutes
Description: Thesis film of Jang Joon-hwan, Bong's classmate at the Korean
Academy of Film Arts. Bong served as the cinematographer.

1996
*Maekchuga aeinboda choŭn ilgopkaji iyu (Seven Reasons Why Beer Is Better
Than a Lover)*
Republic of Korea
Production: Park Chul-soo Films
Producer: Park Chul-soo
Distribution: Cinema Service
Directors: Kim Yu-jin, Jang Hyun-soo, Chung Ji-young, Park Chul-soo, Park
Jong-won, Jang Gil-su, Kang Woo-suk
Screenplay: Kim Yu-min
Adaptation: Byeon Won-mi, Bong Joon Ho
Cinematography: Jeong Han-chul, Kim Hyo-jin, Lee Suk-hyun, Choi Jung-woo,
Jin Yong-hwan, Kwak Myeong-hun
Principal cast: Han Jae-seok, Pang Eun-jin, Sin Hui-jo, Lee Sun-mi
Format: 35 mm, color
109 minutes
Description: Omnibus comedy for which Bong had an adaptation credit. The
film was criticized for its misogyny, and Bong expressed embarrassment over
his participation.

1997
Mot'el sŏninjang (Motel Cactus)
Republic of Korea
Production: Uno Film
Executive producers: Cha Seung-jae, Kim Seung-bum
Producer: Kim Seonah
Director: Park Ki-yong
Screenplay: Park Ki-yong, Bong Joon Ho
Editor: Ham Sung-won
Cinematography: Christopher Doyle
Music: Cho Joon-hyoung
Art direction: Choi Jeong-hwa, Oh Jai-won
Principal cast: Lee Mi-youn, Jin Hee-kyung, Jung Woo-sung, Park Shin-yang
Format: 35 mm, color
90 minutes
Description: Episodic drama consisting of four separate stories that occur in
the same room of a love hotel in Seoul. Bong was one of the screenwriters.

1999
Yuryŏng (Phantom: The Submarine)
Republic of Korea
Production: Uno Film
Executive producer: Cha Seung-jae
Producer: Kim Seonah
Director: Min Byung-chun
Original story: Cha Seung-jae
Screenplay: Jang Joon-hwan, Bong Joon Ho, Kim Jong-hoon
Editor: Go Lim Pyo
Cinematography: Hong Kyung-pyo (Alex Hong)
Music: Lee Dong-jun
Art direction: Hwang In-jun
Principal cast: Choi Min-soo, Jung Woo-sung, Yoon Joo-sang, Son Byung-ho, Go Dong-eop
Format: 35 mm, color
103 minutes
Description: An action movie that takes place on a secret nuclear submarine staffed by crew members who have been recorded as dead in official government documents. Bong was one of the screenwriters.

2002
P'ido nunmulto ŏpshi (No Blood No Tears)
Republic of Korea
Executive producer: Kim Mi-hee
Producer: Kim Seong-je
Distribution: Cinema Service
Director: Ryoo Seung-wan
Screenplay: Jeong Jin-wan, Ryoo Seung-wan
Editors: Kim Sang-bum, Kim Jae-beom
Cinematography: Choi Young-hwan
Music: Han Jae-gwon
Production design: Ryu Seong-hui
Principal cast: Jeon Do-youn, Lee Hye-young, Jung Jae-young, Ryoo Seung-bum, Shin Koo, Bong Joon Ho (cameo)
Format: 35 mm, color
116 minutes
Description: Action crime comedy about two women who come up with a plan to steal money from gangsters. Bong appears in a cameo role as a police detective.

2005
Namgŭgilgi (Antarctic Journal)
Republic of Korea

Production: Sidus
Executive producers: Cha Seung-jae, No Jong-yun
Coexecutive producer: Chae Hui-seung
Producer: Im Hee Chul
Distribution: Showbox Entertainment
Director: Yim Pil-sung
Screenplay: Yim Pil-sung, Bong Joon Ho, Lee Hae-jun
Editor: Kim Sun-min
Cinematography: Chung Chung-hoon
Music: Kenji Kawai
Production design: Hwang In-jun
Principal cast: Song Kang-ho, Yoo Ji-tae, Kim Gyeong-ik, Park Hee-son
Format: 35 mm, color
114 minutes
Description: Survival horror thriller about a polar expedition in Antarctica. Bong
was one of the screenwriters.

2008
Missŭ Hongdangmu (*Crush and Blush*)
Republic of Korea
Production: Moho Film
Executive producer: Park Chan-wook
Producer: Lee Min-su
Distribution: Vantage Holdings
Director: Lee Kyoung-mi
Screenplay: Lee Kyoung-mi, Park Eun-gyo, Park Chan-wook
Editor: Sin Min-gyeong
Cinematography: Kim Dong-young
Music: Jang Young-gyu
Art direction: Hwang Ju-hye
Principal cast: Kong Hyo-jin, Lee Jong-hyuk, Seo U, Hwang-woo Seul-hye,
Pang Eun-jin
Format: 35 mm, color
110 minutes
Description: Comedy about a high school teacher with a propensity for blushing
who has a crush on one of her colleagues. Bong played a small cameo role.

2012
Yŏnghwap'an (*Ari Ari the Korean Cinema*)
Republic of Korea
Production: Aura Pictures
Producers: Heo Chul, Chung Ji-young, Kwack Tae Jun
Distribution: Mountain Pictures

Directors: Heo Chul, Chung Ji-young
Screenplay: Chung Ji-young, Heo Chul
Cinematography: Heo Chul, Chung Ji-young
Principal cast: Yoon Jin-seo, Chung Ji-young
Format: color
83 minutes
Description: Documentary about Korean cinema featuring director Chung
  Ji-young and actress Yoon Jin-seo. Bong Joon Ho is interviewed in the film.

2012
Illyumyŏlmangbogosŏ (Doomsday Book)
Republic of Korea
Production: Zio Entertainment, TimeStory Group
Producers: Choe Hyeon-muk, Jeong Gyeong-u, Kang Young-mo, Kim Jeong-hwa
Distribution: Lotte Entertainment
Directors: Yim Pil-sung, Kim Jee-woon
Screenplay: Yim Pil-sung, Lee Hwan-hui, Kim Jee-woon, Yang Jong-gyu
Editors: Nam Na-young, Kim Mi-yeong
Cinematography: Jo Sang-yuen, Kim Ji-yong, Ha Seong min
Music: Mowg
Art direction: Kang So-young, Cho Hwa-sung, Park Ju-yeong
Principal cast: Ryoo Seung-bun, Go Joon-Hee, Kim Roi-ha, Lee Kan-hee,
  Hwang Hyo-eun
Format: 35 mm, color
113 minutes
Description: Sci-fi anthology film made by directors Yim Pil-sung and Kim
  Jee-woon about the apocalypse. Bong appears in the first of three segments.

2014
Haemoo (Sea Fog)
Republic of Korea
Production: Lewis Pictures, Finecut
Executive producers: Joh Neung-yeon, Kim Tae-wan, Bong Joon Ho
Producers: Yu In-su, Han Sang-beom
Distribution: Next Entertainment World
Director: Shim Sung-bo
Screenplay: Shim Sung-bo, Bong Joon Ho
Editors: Kim Sang-bum, Kim Jae-beom
Cinematography: Alex Hong
Music: Jeong Jae-il
Art direction: Lee Ha-jun
Principal cast: Kim Yoon-suk, Park Yu-cheon, Han Yeri, Moon Sung-keun, Kim
  Sang-ho

Format: 35 mm, color

110 minutes

Description: Drama about the crew of a fishing boat that attempts to smuggle illegal migrants from China to South Korea in dangerous conditions. Bong produced the film and collaborated on the screenplay.

2021

Ponŭn kŏsŭl saranghanda (I Love What I Watch)

Republic of Korea

Distribution: Kim Hak-joong, Lee Jin, Yoon Mi-jeong

Director: Yun Ki-hyoung

Editor: Jeong Jin-hui

Cinematography: Yun Ki-hyoung

Format: color

75 minutes

Description: Documentary about Korean movie theaters in the 1980s, before the advent of large multiplexes, with a special focus on the Aegwan Theater. Bong Joon Ho is interviewed in the documentary.

2023

Noranmun: segimal shinep'il taiŏri (Yellow Door: '90s Lo-Fi Film Club)

Republic of Korea

Production: Broccoli Pictures

Producer: Lee Byungwon

Distribution: Netflix

Director: Lee Hyeok-rae

Editor: Won Chang-jae

Cinematography: Park Hong-yeol

Music: Park Seong-do

Art direction: Han Ju Yea-Seul

Format: color

84 minutes

Description: Documentary about a film club in Seoul in the 1990s. Bong was a founding member of the club and is featured in the film.

Acuna, Angelique. "The Evolution of the Monstrous: An Interview with Bong Joon-Ho." *Film Matters* 12.2 (2021): 119–24.

An, Ji-yoon. "The Korean Mother in Contemporary Thriller Films: A Monster or Just Modern?" *Journal of Japanese and Korean Cinema* 11.2 (2019): 154–69.

Anderson, Perry. *The H-Word: The Peripeteia of Hegemony*. London: Verso, 2017.

Angierski, Kristen. "Superpig Blues: Agribusiness Ecohorror in Bong Joon-ho's *Okja*." In *Fear and Nature: Ecohorror Studies in the Anthropocene*, edited by Christy Tidwell and Carter Soles, 217–36. University Park: Pennsylvania State University Press, 2021.

Arrighi, Giovanni. *The Long Twentieth Century: Money, Power, and the Origins of Our Times*. New ed. London: Verso, 2010.

Asokan, Sue Heun Kim. "Giving Death: The Hero as Sovereign Utility in Bong Joon-Ho's *Snowpiercer* (2013)." *Journal of Japanese and Korean Cinema* 12.2 (2020): 138–52.

Asokan, Sue Heun Kim. "The 'Good' Mother's Self(ish)-Sacrifice: Violence, Redemption, and Deconstructed Ethics in Bong Joon-ho's *Mother* (2009)." *Korea Journal* 61.3 (2021): 223–50.

Barnwell, Jane. "Vertical Hierarchy and the Home in *Parasite*." In *Production Design and the Cinematic Home*, by Jane Barnwell, 23–44. Cham, Switzerland: Springer International, 2022.

Benjamin, Walter. "The Task of the Translator." In *Walter Benjamin: Selected Writing*, vol. 1, *1913–1926*, edited by Marcus Bullock and Michael W. Jennings, 253–63. Cambridge, MA: Belknap Press of Harvard University Press, 1996.

Biles, Jeremy. Review of *Snowpiercer*, directed by Bong Joon Ho. *Religious Studies Review* 40.4 (2014): 218.

Bong, Joon Ho. "Guilty Pleasures: Bong Joon-Ho, Director of *The Host*." *Film Comment* 43.1 (2007): 12.

Bong, Joon Ho. *Parasite: A Graphic Novel in Storyboards*. New York: Grand Central, 2020.

Bose, Nandana. "'Cinematic Comrades': Bong Joon-ho's Auteurism and Song Kang-ho's Performance." *Senses of Cinema* 98 (2021). http://www.sensesof cinema.com/2021/feature-articles/cinematic-comrades.

Brinkhof, Tim. "The Surprisingly Conservative Gender Politics of Parasite." *Off-screen* 25.2–3 (2021). https://offscreen.com/view/the-surprisingly-conservative-gender-politics-of-parasite.

Brouillette, Sarah, Joshua Clover, and Annie McClanahan. "Late, Autumnal, Immiserating, Terminal." *Theory and Event* 22.2 (2019): 325–36.

Buder, Emily. "How the 'Okja' VFX Team Created the Creature That Turned Us All Vegetarian." *No Film School*, July 12, 2017. https://nofilmschool.com/2017/07/vfx-okja-erik-jan-de-boer-interview.

Canavan, Gerry. "'If the Engine Ever Stops, We'd All Die': *Snowpiercer* and Necrofuturism." *Paradoxa: Studies in World Literary Genres* 26 (2014): 41–66.

Chang, Kyung-Sup. "Compressed Modernity and Its Discontents: South Korean Society in Transition." *Economy and Society* 28.1 (1999): 30–55.

Chang, Kyung-Sup. *South Korea under Compressed Modernity: Familial Political Economy in Transition.* London: Routledge, 2010.

Cho, Michelle. "Face Value: The Star as Genre in Bong Joon-ho's *Mother.*" In *The Korean Popular Culture Reader*, edited by Kyung Hyun Kim and Youngmin Choe, 168–93. Durham, NC: Duke University Press, 2014.

Cho, Michelle. "K-Crossover, or, Crying over Marbles." *The Hallyu Project*, Post45, Feb. 23, 2023. https://post45.org/2023/02/k-crossover-or-crying-over-marbles/.

Choe, Youngmin. *Tourist Distractions: Traveling and Feeling in Transnational Hallyu Cinema.* Durham, NC: Duke University Press, 2016.

Choi, Chungmoo. *Healing Historical Trauma in South Korean Film and Literature.* London: Routledge, 2021.

Choi, Jinhee. *The South Korean Film Renaissance: Local Hitmakers, Global Provocateurs.* Middletown, CT: Wesleyan University Press, 2010.

Christensen, Jerome. *America's Corporate Art: The Studio Authorship of Hollywood Motion Pictures.* Stanford, CA: Stanford University Press, 2011.

Chu, Kiu-wai. "Bong Joon-ho's *Snowpiercer* (2014)—Adventure Cli-Fi." In *Cli-Fi: A Companion*, edited by Axel Goodbody and Adeline Johns-Putra, 73–80. Oxford: Peter Lang, 2018.

Chung, Hye Seung, and David Scott Diffrient. *Movie Migrations: Transnational Genre Flows and South Korean Cinema.* New Brunswick, NJ: Rutgers University Press, 2015.

Connor, J. D. *The Studios after the Studios: Neoclassical Hollywood (1970–2010).* Stanford, CA: Stanford University Press, 2015.

Cooper, Melinda. *Family Values: Between Neoliberalism and the New Social Conservatism.* New York: Zone Books, 2017.

Cooper, Melinda. "Secular Stagnation: Fear of a Non-Reproductive Future." *Postmodern Culture* 27.1 (2016). https://www.pomoculture.org/2020/09/21/secular.

Corrigan, Timothy. "The Commerce of Auteurism: A Voice without Authority." *New German Critique* 49 (1990): 43–57.

Coyle, Jake. "Fall Preview: Bong Joon Ho and 'Parasite' Are Coming for You." AP News, Aug. 28, 2019. https://apnews.com/963f3e97df5a42e79b327585e7fec603.

Cumings, Bruce. "The Korean Crisis and the End of 'Late' Development." *New Left Review* 231 (1998): 43–72.

Doo, Rumy. "Bong Joon-ho Speaks Up on 'Okja' Controversy." *Korea Herald*, June 14, 2017. https://www.koreaherald.com/view.php?ud=20170614000733.

Ďurovičová, Nataša, and Garrett Stewart. "Amnesias of Murder: *Mother*." *Film Quarterly* 64.2 (2010): 64–68.

Ebbighausen, Rodion. "South Korea and Germany Share Same Geopolitical Dilemma." DW, May 8, 2023. https://www.dw.com/en/a-65553998.

Farahbakhsh, Alireza, and Ramtin Ebrahimi. "The Social Implications of Metaphor in Bong Joon-Ho's *Parasite*." *CINEJ Cinema Journal* 9.1 (2021): 87–116.

Gabilondo, Joseba. "Bong Joon Ho's *Parasite* and Post-2008 Revolts: From the Discourse of the Master to the Destituent Power of the Real." *International Journal of Zizek Studies* 14.1 (2020): 1–20.

Garrett, Daniel. "The Cosmopolitan Perspective, the Rebellious Impulse: *The Matrix* Trilogy and *Snowpiercer* (Part 1)." *Offscreen* 20.1 (2016). https://offscreen.com/view/the-cosmopolitan-perspective-pt1.

Gide, André. *Journal 1889–1939*. Translated by Justin O'Brien. New York: Penguin, 1984.

Gilliam, Carey. "Timeline: History of Monsanto Co." *Reuters*, Nov. 10, 2009. https://www.reuters.com/article/us-food-monsanto/idUSTRE5AA05Q20091111.

Gorbman, Claudia. "Bong's Song." *Film Quarterly* 71.3 (2018): 21–26.

Haraway, Donna. "Situated Knowledges: The Science Question in Feminism and the Privilege of Partial Perspective." *Feminist Studies* 14.3 (1988): 575–99.

Harris, Bryan. "Why South Korea Risks Following Japan into Economic Stagnation." *Financial Review*, Aug. 21, 2018. https://www.afr.com/world/why-south-korea-risks-following-japan-into-economic-stagnation-20180821-h1491c.

Harvey, David. "The Geography of Capitalist Accumulation: A Reconstruction of the Marxian Theory." *Antipode* 7.2 (1975): 9–21.

Harvey, David. "Neo-Liberalism as Creative Destruction." *Geografiska Annaler: Series B, Human Geography* 88.2 (2006): 145–58.

Held, David. "At the Global Crossroads: The End of the Washington Consensus and the Rise of Global Social Democracy?" *Globalizations* 2.1 (2005): 95–113.

Holub, Christian. "*Parasite* Director Bong Joon Ho Discussing the Film's Twisty Ending." *Entertainment Weekly*, Oct. 23, 2019. https://ew.com/movies/2019/10/23/parasite-bong-joon-ho-ending-explained/.

"*The Host* (2006)." Box Office Mojo by IMDbPro. https://www.boxofficemojo.com/title/tt0468492/; accessed May 12, 2023.

Hsu, Hsuan. "The Dangers of Biosecurity: *The Host* and the Geopolitics of Outbreak." *Jump Cut* 51 (2009). https://www.ejumpcut.org/archive/jc51.2009/Host/text.html.

Hsu, Hsuan. *The Scent of Risk: Environmental Disparities and Olfactory Aesthetics*. New York: New York University Press, 2020.

Hutcheon, Linda. *A Theory of Parody: The Teachings of Twentieth-Century Art Forms*. Champaign: University of Illinois Press, 2000.

Hwang, Yŏngmi, and Kim Simu. *Pong Chunhorŭl ikta* [Reading Bong Joon Ho]. Seoul: Seoul, 2020.

I Hyŏngsŏk. *Kyehoegi ta issŏttŏn namja, Pong Chunho* [A Man with a Plan, Bong Joon Ho]. Seoul: Book Ocean, 2020.

Im U-gi. *Han'gukyŏnghwa segamdok, I Ch'angtong, Hong Sangsu, Pong Chunho* [Three Korean Film Directors, Lee Chang-dong, Hong Sang-su, Bong Joon Ho]. Seoul: Seoul, 2021.

Imanjaya, E., A. Amelia, and Meilani. "Three 'Ecological Monsters' in Bong Joon-Ho's Films." *IOP Conference Series: Earth and Environmental Science* 729.1 (2021). https://doi.org/10.1088/1755-1315/729/1/012103.

I Sangyong. *Pong Chunhoŭi yŏnghwa ŏnŏ* [Bong Joon Ho's Film Language]. Paju: Nanda, 2021.

Iwabuchi, Koichi. *Recentering Globalization: Popular Culture and Japanese Transnationalism*. Durham, NC: Duke University Press, 2002.

Iwai, Yoshiko. "Narrative Humility and *Parasite*, Directed by Bong Joon Ho, 2019." *Journal of Medical Humanities* 43.1 (2020): 197–99.

I Yongch'ŏl, I Hyŏnkyŏng, and Chŏng Mina. *Pong Chunho k'odŭ* [Bong Joon Ho Code]. Seoul: Midas Books, 2022.

Jagoda, Patrick. *Experimental Games: Critique, Play, and Design in the Age of Gamification*. Chicago: University of Chicago Press, 2020.

Jameson, Fredric. "Postmodernism, or the Cultural Logic of Late Capitalism." *New Left Review* 146 (1989): 59–92.

Jeon, Joseph Jonghyun. "Lines Left to Cross: Deglobalization and the Domestic Western in Bong Joon-ho's *Parasite*." *Critical Inquiry* 49.4 (2023): 557–80.

Jeon, Joseph Jonghyun. "Memories of Memories: Historicity, Nostalgia, and Archive in Bong Joon-ho's 'Memories of Murder.'" *Cinema Journal* 51.1 (2011): 75–95.

Jeon, Joseph Jonghyun. "Neoliberal Forms: CGI, Algorithm, and Hegemony in Korea's IMF Cinema." *Representations* 126.1 (2014): 85–111.

Jeon, Joseph Jonghyun. *Vicious Circuits: Korea's IMF Cinema and the End of the American Century*. Stanford, CA: Stanford University Press, 2019.

Jeon Chanil. *Pong Chunho, Changnŭga toen kamdok* [Bong Joon Ho, the Director That Became a Genre]. Seoul: Chakka, 2020.

Jeong, Kelly Y. "Gender and Class in *Parasite*." In *The Soft Power of the Korean Wave: "Parasite," BTS, and Drama*, edited by Youna Kim, 79–89. London: Routledge, 2021.

Jeong, Seung-hoon. "*Snowpiercer* (2013): The Post-Historical Catastrophe of a Biopolitical Ecosystem." In *Rediscovering Korean Cinema*, edited by Sangjoon Lee, 486–501. Ann Arbor: University of Michigan Press, 2019.

Jin, Dal Yong. *Transnational Korean Cinema: Cultural Politics, Film Genres, and Digital Technologies*. New Brunswick, NJ: Rutgers University Press, 2019.

Jung, E. Alex. "The House That *Parasite* Built (from Scratch)." *Vulture*, Feb. 4, 2020, https://www.vulture.com/2020/02/how-bong-joon-ho-built-the-houses-in-parasite.html.

Jung, Ji-youn. *Korean Film Directors: Bong Joon-ho*. Translated by Colin A. Mouat. Seoul: Seoul Selection, 2008.

Kiaer, Jieun, and Loli Kim. "One-Inch-Tall Barrier of Subtitles: Translating Invisibility in *Parasite*." In *The Soft Power of the Korean Wave: "Parasite," BTS, and Drama*, edited by Youna Kim, 90–103. London: Routledge, 2021.

Kim, Dong Hoon. "Producers of *Parasite* and the Question of Film Authorship: Producing a Global Author, Authoring a Global Production." In *The Soft Power of the Korean Wave: "Parasite," BTS, and Drama*, edited by Youna Kim, 41–53. London: Routledge, 2021.

Kim, Kyung Hyun. *Hegemonic Mimicry: Korean Popular Culture of the Twenty-First Century*. Durham, NC: Duke University Press, 2021.

Kim, Kyung Hyun. *The Remasculinization of Korean Cinema*. Durham, NC: Duke University Press, 2004.

Kim, Kyung Hyun. *Virtual Hallyu: Korean Cinema of the Global Era*. Durham, NC: Duke University Press, 2011.

Kim, Kyung Hyun, and Youngmin Choe, editors. *The Korean Popular Culture Reader*. Durham, NC: Duke University Press, 2014.

Kim, Se-young. "Surviving Digital Asia: *PlayerUnknown's Battlegrounds* and the Affective Economy of the Battle Royale." *Verge: Studies in Global Asias* 7.2 (2021): 128–50.

Kim, Suhyun. "(In)Commensurability of Korean Cinema: International Coproduction of Korean Films in the 2010s." *Korea Journal* 59.4 (2019): 136–66.

Kim Hyun Ah. "Pong Chunho yŏnghwae nat'anan konggan'gwa rok'ŏllit'i: *Sarinŭi ch'uŏk, Koemul, Kisaengch'ung* ŭl chungshimŭro" [The Representation of Space and Locality in Bong Joon Ho's Films]. *Munhakkwa yŏngsang* [Literature and Film] 21.2 (2020): 249–78.

Kim Sangmin. "Han'gukyŏnghwaŭi kŭllobŏllaijeisyŏn (globalization) e kwanhan shironjŏk yŏn'gu'—Pak Ch'anukkwa Pong Chunhoŭi chaehyŏnjŏllyakŭl chungshimŭro" [A Study on Globalization of Korean Cinema—Focusing on the Representation Strategy of Park Chan-wook and Bong Joon Ho]. *Sai* [Sai] 31 (2021): 393–430.

Klein, Christina. "Why American Studies Needs to Think about Korean Cinema, or, Transnational Genres in the Films of Bong Joon-Ho." *American Quarterly* 60.4 (2008): 871–98.

Koreaboo. "Koreans Discovered How Much Won Bin Makes from CFs and It Blew Their Minds." July 9, 2018. https://www.koreaboo.com/news/koreans-discovered.

Ku, Robert. *Dubious Gastronomy: The Cultural Politics of Eating Asian in the USA*. Honolulu: University of Hawai'i Press, 2014.

Kwon, Jake, and Julia Hollingsworth. "South Korean Man Confesses to a Series of Murders That Stumped Police for Decades." *CNN*, Oct. 4, 2019. https://www.cnn.com/2019/10/04/asia/south-korean-serial-murder-confessed-intl -hnk-scli/index.html.

Lechini, Gladys. Introduction to *Globalization and the Washington Consensus: Its Influence on Democracy and Development in the South*, edited by Gladys Lechini, 9–24. Buenos Aires: CLASCO, 2008.

Lee, Dong-Hoo. "Transnational Film Project in the Changing Media Ecology: The Case of *Okja*." In *Asia-Pacific Film Co-Productions: Theory, Industry and Aesthetics*, edited by Dal Yong Jin and Wendy Su, 155–76. London: Routledge, 2020.

Lee, Fred, and Steven Manicastri. "Not All Are Aboard: Decolonizing Exodus in Joon-Ho Bong's *Snowpiercer*." *New Political Science* 40.2 (2018): 211–26.

Lee, Kevin B. "The Han River Horror Show: Interview with Bong Joon-ho." *Cineaste* 32.2 (2007). https://www.cineaste.com/spring2007/interview-with -bong-joon-ho.

Lee, Meera. "Monstrosity and Humanity in Bong Joon-Ho's *The Host*." *Positions: East Asia Cultures Critique* 26.4 (2018): 719–47.

Lee, Nam. *The Films of Bong Joon Ho*. New Brunswick, NJ: Rutgers University Press, 2020.

Lee, Nikki Ji Yeon. "Localized Globalization and a Monster National: 'The Host' and the South Korean Film Industry." *Cinema Journal* 50.3 (2011): 45–61.

Lee, Nikki Ji Yeon, and Julian Stringer. "From Screenwriting for Sound to Film Sound Maps: The Evolution of Live Tone's Creative Alliance with Bong Joon-Ho." *New Soundtrack* 8.2 (2018): 145–59.

Lee, Sangjoon. *Cinema and the Cultural Cold War: U.S. Diplomacy and the Origins of the Asian Cinema Network*. Ithaca, NY: Cornell University Press, 2020.

Lee, Sangjoon, editor. *Rediscovering Korean Cinema*. Ann Arbor: University of Michigan Press, 2019.

Lee Chan. "Pong Chunho yŏnghwaŭi modŏnit'i inshikkwa kongjonŭi yullihang— *P'ŭllandasŭŭi kae, Kisaengch'ung* ŭl chungshimŭro" [The Perception of Modernity and Ethics of Coexistence in Bong Joon Ho's movies *Barking Dogs Never Bite* and *Parasite*]. *Pigyomunhwayŏn'gu* [Comparative Cultural Studies] 61 (2020): 331–67.

Lee Nam. "Pong Chunhoŭi yŏnghwa *Sŏlgukyŏlch'a* (2013) wa *Kisaengch'ung* (2019) e nat'ananŭn kyegŭp yanggŭk'hwawa p'agukchŏk sangsangnyŏk" [Class Polarization and Catastrophic Imagination in Bong Joon Ho's *Snowpiercer* (2013) and *Parasite* (2019)]. *Tisŭp'ojit'ip'ŭ* [Dispositive] 8 (2021): 139–54.

Lim, Eng-Beng. "Living in *Parasite* Country as an Asian/American." *Los Angeles Review of Books*, Feb. 24, 2020. https://blog.lareviewofbooks.org/essays/ living-parasite/.

Lindsay, Benjamin. "Bong Joon-Ho, 'Parasite' Writer and Director." *Backstage* 60.29 (2019): 18.

Lukasiak, Beata. *"The Host*: The Monster Emerging from the *Han."* *Senses of Cinema* 68 (2013). http://www.sensesofcinema.com/2013/cteq/the-host.

Magnier, Mark. "Yoshiaki Shiraishi; Founded Conveyor Belt Sushi Industry." *Los Angeles Times*, Sept. 2, 2001. https://www.latimes.com/archives/la-xpm-2001-sep-02-me-41354-story.html.

Martin, Theodore. *Contemporary Drift: Genre, Historicism, and the Problem of the Present.* New York: Columbia University Press, 2017.

Marx, Karl. *Capital.* Vol. 1. New York: Penguin, 1990.

McClanahan, Annie. "Serious Crises: Rethinking the Neoliberal Subject." *boundary 2* 46.1 (2019): 103–32.

McHugh, Kathleen. "South Korean Film Melodrama: State, Nation, Woman, and the Transnational Familiar." In *South Korean Golden Age Melodrama: Gender, Genre, and National Cinema*, edited by Kathleen McHugh and Nancy Abelmann, 17–42. Detroit, MI: Wayne State University Press, 2005.

Menne, Jeff. *Post-Fordist Cinema: Hollywood Auteurs and the Corporate Counterculture.* New York: Columbia University Press, 2019.

Moon, Criss, and Julie Moon. "'Parasite' and the Plurality of Empire." *Public Books*, June 23, 2020. https://www.publicbooks.org/parasite-and-the-plurality-of-empire/.

Moon So-jeong. "Han'guk kajokpyŏndongŭi yŏksajŏk maengnagesŏ sangsanghan *Madŏ* ŭi kajokyongmang" [Rethinking *Mother* in the Historical Context of the Korean Family]. *Yŏsŏnghakyŏn'gu* [Journal of Women's Studies] 20 (2010): 97–118.

Moon So-young. "Pong Chunho yŏnghwa *Kisaengch'unggwa Sŏlgukyŏlch'aŭi* sangjingjŏng kongganŭl t'onghae nat'anan chonggyorosŏŭi chabonjuŭi" [Capitalism as Religion Unfolded through the Symbolic Spaces of Bong Joon Ho's Film *Parasite* in Comparison with His *Snowpiercer*]. *Yesulgwa Midiŏ* [Arts and Media] 19.2 (2020): 151–76.

Moretti, Franco. *Signs Taken for Wonders: On the Sociology of Literary Forms.* London: Verso, 1983.

Neale, Stephen. *Genre.* London: British Film Institute, 1980.

Noh, Jean. "Bong Joon Ho, Ryusuke Hamaguchi Talk Influences, Casting and Shooting in Cars." *Screen International*, Oct. 8, 2021. https://www.proquest.com/docview/2580338884.

Noh, Jean. "Bong Joon Ho, *Snowpiercer*." *Screen International*, Aug. 29, 2013. https://www.proquest.com/docview/1428655416/.

Noh, Jean. "Bong Joon Ho Talks 'Parasite': 'It Deals with Polarisation.'" *Screen International*, May 17, 2019. https://www.proquest.com/docview/2226783548.

Noh, Jean. "'Okja' Director Bong Joon Ho Talks Cannes Competition, Netflix." *Screen International*, May 17, 2017. https://www.proquest.com/docview/1899777752.

Noh, Minjung. "*Parasite* as Parable: Bong Joon-Ho's Cinematic Capitalism." *Cross Currents* 70.3 (2020): 248–62.

OED (Oxford English Dictionary). "parody, n." https://www.oed.com/dictionary/parody_n1/; accessed February 4, 2024.

Oh, Yoon Jeong. "The Transcultural Logic of Capital: The House and Stairs in *Parasite*." In *The Soft Power of the Korean Wave: "Parasite," BTS, and Drama*, edited by Youna Kim, 67–78. London: Routledge, 2021.

Orlov, Alex. "Should Any Piece of Sushi Take Five Flights? A Restaurant Group Takes on the Future of Fish." *Mic*, July 28, 2017. https://www.mic.com/articles/182570/should-any-piece-of-sushi-take-five-flights-a-restaurant-group-takes-on-the-future-of-fish.

Paik, Peter. "*The Host* (2006): Life in Excess." In *Rediscovering Korean Cinema*, edited by Sangjoon Lee, 423–34. Ann Arbor: University of Michigan Press, 2019.

Pak, Chinhu, and Taekŭn Im. "Pong Chun-ho changnйŭi kanŭngsŏng: *Kisaengch'ung* ŭi k'ŭrono'op'ŭ sŏsajŏllyak" [The Possibility of 'Bong Joon Ho Genre': Chronotope Narrative Strategy of the Film *Parasite*]. *Yŏnghwayŏngu* [Film Studies] 84 (2020): 61–87.

Paquet, Darcy. *New Korean Cinema: Breaking the Waves*. London: Wallflower, 2009.

"Parasite (2019)." Box Office Mojo by IMDbPro. https://www.boxofficemojo.com/title/tt6751668/; accessed May 12, 2023.

Park, Ed. "The Bong Show: Bong Joon-Ho." In *Exile Cinema: Filmmakers at Work beyond Hollywood*, edited by Michael Atkinson, 49–54. Albany: State University of New York Press, 2008.

Peter, Laurence. "German Protest over Pig Patent." *BBC News*, Apr. 16, 2009. http://news.bbc.co.uk/2/hi/europe/8002503.stm.

Pettigrew, Ian. Review of *Snowpiercer*, directed by Bong Joon Ho. *Science Fiction Film and Television* 9.1 (2016): 150–53.

Rayns, Tony. "The Makings of Bong Joon Ho." *Sight and Sound*, Feb. 12, 2020. https://www2.bfi.org.uk/news-opinion/sight-sound-magazine/interviews/bong-joon-ho-career-story.

San Juan, E., Jr. "Crisis and Contradiction in Globalization Discourse." *Red Critique* 11 (2006). http://www.redcritique.org/WinterSpring2006/.

Schulze, Joshua. "The Sacred Engine and the Rice Paddy: Globalization, Genre, and Local Space in the Films of Bong Joon-Ho." *Journal of Popular Film and Television* 47.1 (2019): 21–29.

Seo Jeong-nam. "Yŏnghwa *Sŏlgukyŏlch'a* wa Pong Chun-hoŭi sŏsajŏllyak-allegorijŏk sŏnghyangŭl kajin inmul k'aerikt'ŏŭi susahak" [The Film *Snowpiercer* and Narrative Strategies of Director Bong Joon Ho: Rhetoric of Characters with Allegorical Inclinations]. *Han'gungmunhagiron'gwa Pi'yŏng* [Korean Literary Theory and Criticism] 68 (2015): 33–66.

Shackleton, Liz. "Quentin Tarantino and Bong Joon Ho in Conversation." *Screen Daily*, Oct. 11, 2013. https://www.screendaily.com/news/5062432.article.

Sharf, Zach. "Bong Joon Ho Duped Harvey Weinstein with a Hilarious Lie to Save 'Snowpiercer' Scene." *IndieWire*, Oct. 8, 2019. https://www.indiewire.com/features/general/bong-joon-ho-battles-harvey-weinstein-snowpiercer-final-cut-1202179635/.

Shin, Chi-Yun, and Julian Stringer, editors. *New Korean Cinema*. New York: New York University Press, 2005.

Shin, Ji-hye. "Ha-Joon Chang Says, 'No Welfare, No Growth.'" *Korea Industry and Technology Times*, Jan. 3, 2013. http://www.koreaittimes.com/news/articleView.html?idxno=25428.

Smith, Neil. *Uneven Development: Nature, Capital, and the Production of Space*. 3rd ed. Athens: University of Georgia Press, 2008.

Sohn, Hee-jeong, and Yijung Jung. "Gender in 'Korean Reality': Bong Joon-Ho's Films and the Birth of 'Snob Film.'" *Azalea: Journal of Korean Literature and Culture* 14 (2021): 289–310.

Sontag, Susan. *Against Interpretation and Other Essays*. New York: Farrar, Straus, and Giroux, 1966.

Summers, Lawrence H. "The Age of Secular Stagnation: What It Is and What to Do about It." *Foreign Affairs* 95.2 (2016): 2–9.

Sung, Jinsoo. "Tongshidae han'gukyŏnghwaesŏ chakkajuŭiŭi sangŏpchŏk suyong yangsang" [The Commerce of Auteurism in Contemporary Korean Films]. *Yŏnghwayŏngu* [Film Studies] 63 (2015): 161–94.

Szalay, Michael. *Second Lives: Black-Market Melodrama and the Reinvention of Television*. Chicago: University of Chicago Press, 2023.

Tanaka, Motoko. "Trends of Fiction in 2000s Japanese Pop Culture." *Electronic Journal of Contemporary Japanese Studies* 14.2 (2014). http://www.japanesestudies.org.uk/ejcjs/vol14/iss2/tanaka.html.

Taylor, Brandon. "The Ideological Train to Globalization: Bong Joon-Ho's *The Host* and *Snowpiercer*." *Cineaction!* 98 (2016): 44–48.

Tiffany, Kaitlyn. "Netflix Booed at *Okja*'s Cannes Premiere." *Verge*, May 19, 2017. https://www.theverge.com/2017/5/19/15662542/.

Tweedie, James. *The Age of New Waves: Art Cinema and the Staging of Globalization*. New York: Oxford University Press, 2013.

Uzuner, Nagehan. "Bong Joon Ho, *Okja* (2017): Wounding the Feelings." *Markets, Globalization and Development Review* 5.2 (2020). https://digitalcommons.uri.edu/mgdr/vol5/iss2/7.

Vineyard, Jennifer. "Director Bong Joon-Ho Explains Harvey Weinstein's Problem with *Snowpiercer*." *Vulture*, Nov. 6, 2013. https://www.vulture.com/2013/11/whats-weinsteins-problem-with-snowpiercer.html.

Wade, Robert, and Frank Veneroso. "The Asian Crisis: The High Debt Model versus the Wall Street-Treasury-IMF Complex." *New Left Review* 228 (1998): 3–23.

Wagner, Keith B. "A Jamesonian Reading of *Parasite* (2019): Homes, Real Estate Speculation, and Bubble Markets in Seoul." In *Fredric Jameson and Film Theory: Marxism, Allegory, and Geopolitics in World Cinema*, edited by Keith B. Wagner, Jeremi Szaniawski, and Michael Cramer, 146–64. New Brunswick, NJ: Rutgers University Press, 2022.

Wald, Priscilla. *Contagious: Cultures, Carriers, and the Outbreak Narrative.* Durham, NC: Duke University Press, 2008.

Wallace, Rachel. "Inside the House from Bong Joon Ho's *Parasite.*" *Architectural Digest*, Oct. 31, 2019. https://www.architecturaldigest.com/story/bong-joon -ho-parasite-movie-set-design-interview.

Wall Street Journal. "Why Fried Chicken Is Battering South Korea's Economy." Sept. 13, 2013. Video, 2:54. https://www.wsj.com/video/why-fried-chicken -is-battering-south-korea-economy/9E1C251D-BCC5–4322-BC3F-A07 CoCA7CoB4.html.

Wark, McKenzie. *Gamer Theory.* Cambridge, MA: Harvard University Press, 2007.

White, E. B. *Charlotte's Web.* New York: Harper and Brothers, 1952.

Williams, Raymond. *The Country and the City.* Oxford: Oxford University Press, 1973.

Wilson, Rob. "*Snowpiercer* as Anthropoetics: Killer Capitalism, the Anthropocene, Korean-Global Film." *Boundary 2* 46.3 (2019): 199–218.

Wise, Damon. "Interview: 'Snowpiercer' Director Bong Joon-Ho." *Financial Times*, June 20, 2014. https://www.ft.com/content/4377d830-f61a-11e3-83d3 -00144feabdco.

Wise, Dennis Wilson. Review of *Okja*, directed by Bong Joon Ho. *Science Fiction Film and Television* 12.2 (2019): 290–94.

Wojcik, Pamela Robertson. *The Apartment Plot: Urban Living in American Film and Popular Culture, 1945–1975.* Durham, NC: Duke University Press, 2010.

Yamada, Marc. *Locating Heisei in Japanese Fiction and Film: The Historical Imagination of the Lost Decades.* London: Routledge, 2019.

Yecies, Brian, and Aegyung Shim. *The Changing Face of Korean Cinema, 1960–2015.* London: Routledge, 2016.

Yoo, Sang-Keun. "Necropolitical Metamorphoses: Bong Joon-Ho's *The Host* and *Parasite.*" *Science Fiction Film and Television* 14.1 (2021): 45–69.

Yoon, John. "In K-Pop's Quest for Global Growth, Korean Fans Feel Cast Aside." *New York Times*, Apr. 5, 2023. https://www.nytimes.com/2023/04/04/business/ sm-entertainment-kakao-hybe-kpop.html.

Chang Kyung-sup: on compressed
  modernity, 15, 18–19
Charlotte's Web, 79, 83
Cho, Michelle, 103, 107n12
Cho Yeo-jeong, 95
Choi, Jinhee, 11, 18–19
Choi, Sharon, 111, *130*
Choi Woo-shik, 82, 91
Christensen, Jerome, 10–11
Chun Doo-hwan, 40–41, 118, 120
Chung, Hye Seung, 11
Chung, Lee Isaac, 116–17
Citizen Kane: mise en abyme in, 7, *8*, 9–10
class: in *Barking Dogs Never Bite*, 42; in
  Bong's films, 10, 126; in Korean film,
  89–90; in *Mickey 17*, 105; in *Parasite*,
  89–90, 108n24; in *Snowpiercer*, 10, 105
Cold War, 14; as *Parasite* trope, 23, 87,
  103; South Korea as US client state, 18,
  24, 49, 88
competition: in *Barking Dogs Never Bite*,
  34; global, 87–88, 89; in *Memories of
  Murder*, 28; in *Okja*, 63, 64, 65–66, 68,
  72, 80–82; in *Parasite*, 87–88, 90–91,
  93–94, 96–100, 102; in *Snowpiercer*,
  63, 64, 65–66, 68, 72
Connor, J. D., 11
Corrigan, Timothy, 5, 10
CSI: Crime Scene Investigation, 35, 118
Cure, 119

Dano, Paul, 67
de Boer, Erik-Jan, 82
detective fictions: epistemology of, 25–26;
  locked-room mysteries, 35–36; red
  herrings, 37–38
Diffrient, David Scott, 11
Douglas, John, 119

empire, US, 50–51, 53; US as bad father,
  45
entanglements, 1–2; in Bong's films, 21,
  43, 58, 104; of globalization, 3–4; mise
  en abyme and, 12–13; mise-en-scène
  and, 5, 10, 12; of modernization, 2–4;
  in *Mother*, 2, 4, 6–7, 12, 62
escape, 93, 106; in *Barking Dogs Never
  Bite*, 30, 33; battle royal and, 96; inside,

86–88, 106; *Mother* and, 60, 65; in
  Okja, 63, 65, 77, 84, 86; in *Parasite*, 86;
  in *Snowpiercer*, 63, 75, 76–77, 84, 86
Evans, Chris, 3, 9, 104–5

family and kinship, 106; in *The Host*,
  43–44, 48, 85; idealization of, 43; in
  Mother, 43–44; in *Okja*, 85; in outbreak
  narratives, 52; in *Parasite*, 92, 108n25;
  in *Snowpiercer*, 85; workers as, 89
film: French New Wave, 5–6, 11; global
  New Wave, 2; outbreak narratives, 52;
  transition to digital, 126–27
film, Korean, 114; class in, 89–90; IMF
  Cinema, 49; Korean New Wave, 16,
  18–19, 58; New Korean Cinema,
  18–19; periodization of, 18–19. *See also
  individual films*
film industry, Hollywood, 5, 11, 17, 104
film industry, Korean: Chungmuro
  system, 16; domestic films, 16;
  international distribution markets, 11,
  64, 107n14; neocolonialism and, 17–18;
  Snowpiercer and, 127
Ford, John, 117
French New Wave, 5, 11; mise-en-scène
  in, 5–6
From Hell (Moore graphic novel), 120

Gabilondo, Joseba, 108n24
gamification in, 96, 109n28
Gap-dong (Kaptongi), 36
gender: nationalism and, 58; in postwar
  US, 43
genre: allegory and, 45; battle royal,
  91, 95–100, 109n29; in Bong's films,
  20; confidence game, 91–96; genre-
  bending, 20; Korean melodrama,
  53, 58–59; monster movies, 45, 52;
  outbreak narratives, 52; in *Parasite*,
  91–100, 108n25; police procedurals, 8;
  sabaibukei, 96
Gide, André, 7, 9
globalization: agency and, 103; in
  Bong's films, 2–3; culture and, 2;
  entanglements of, 3–4; parody and,
  68, 83; South Korea and, 87–88; space
  and, 12

Memories of Murder (*Sarinŭi Ch'uŏk*) (*continued*): mise en abyme in, 8–9, 22; mise-en-scène of, 4, 19–20, 22, 22; modernity and, 19–20, 25, 29, 36; police in, 8, 28, 35–40, 46, 54; red herrings in, 37–38; re-enactment in, 37; settings of, 113; social relations in, 43; state violence in, 39; water and rain in, 106, 116; witnessing in, 39–41

Menne, Jeff, 11

Mickey 17, 104–6; production of, 104–5

Minari, 116–17

Mindhunter (Douglas book), 119–20

Miramax: Mirando as stand-in for, 79. *See also* Weinstein Company

mise en abyme: in Bong films, 7–10, 12–13, 42; in *Citizen Kane*, 7, 8, 9–10; compared to mise-en-scène, 10; in *Mickey 17*, 106; in *Memories of Murder*, 8–9, 22; in *Mother*, 7, 7–8, 9, 12, 101–2, 103; in *Parasite*, 86, 92, 103; in *Snowpiercer*, 9–10, 70

mise-en-scène: of *Barking Dogs Never Bite*, 4, 14–15; of Bong's films, 4–5, 12–13, 14–15, 19–22; compared to mise en abyme, 10; defined, 4; entanglements and, 5, 10, 12; in French New Wave films, 5–6; of *Memories of Murder*, 4, 19–20, 22, 22; of *Mickey 17*, 106; of *Mother*, 4–6, 12, 54–55, 62, 64, 101–2; of *Okja*, 77; of *Parasite*, 5, 23, 24, 32, 73, 86–87, 90, 103; place and, 12–13; of "Shaking Tokyo," 42; of *Snowpiercer*, 4–5, 72–73; space and, 12–13

modernity: *Barking Dogs Never Bite* and, 19–20, 25, 29, 31–34, 107n2; in Bong's films, 19–20; capitalism and, 5; compressed, 15, 16, 18–19, 24, 25–26, 29, 43, 46; consumption and, 5; of French New Wave, 5; irresolution of, 25; *Memories of Murder* and, 19–20, 25, 29, 36; *Mother* and, 46; tradition and, 4; uncertainties of, 29; US hegemonic power and, 3; vexed, 31–34

modernization: apartment complexes and, 31–33; in Bong's films, 2–3, 46; disappointments of, 32; entanglements

of, 3–4; in *Okja*, 45; in *Snowpiercer*, 45; of South Korea, 2–3, 15–16, 18–21, 87

Money, 124

Monsanto, 78–79

Motel Cactus, 128

Mother (*Madŏ*), 1–2, 3; as anomalous, 59–60; atemporal juxtaposition in, 61–62; capitalist exchange in, 55–58, 56, 123–25; claustrophobic protectionism of, 4, 24, 46, 59–60, 62–63, 64, 68; development of, 121–22; domestic nationalism in, 62–63; editing of, 60–62; escape and, 60, 65; failed parenting in, 44–45, 47, 52, 62, 64; family in, 43–44; globalization and, 63; golf course scene, 53, 56, 59, 123; jail scene, 2–3, 4–5, 6, 12, 103; justice in, 1, 57, 63; memory in, 58–59, 60–62; mise en abyme in, 7, 7–8, 9, 12, 101–2, 103; mise-en-scène of, 4–6, 12, 54–55, 62, 64, 101–2; modernity and, 46; police in, 54, 118; settings of, 113; small-town dynamics in, 14, 46, 54–55, 64, 121–22; social entanglements in, 2, 4, 6–7, 12, 62; social reproduction in, 102; space in, 102; spatial and temporal dislocations in, 13; tight framing in, 52–54, 53, 58, 59–60, 64; violence in, 55; water and rain in, 106, 116

nationalism: domestic, 58, 62–63; gender and, 58

nationhood: domestic, 86–87; in *Parasite*, 87

Neale, Stephen, 108n25

neocolonialism, 50, 59; Korean film industry and, 17–18

neoliberalism, 88; gamification and, 109n28; South Korea and, 19; Washington Consensus, 17

Netflix, 64, 79

New Korean Cinema, 18–19

Okja (*Okcha*), 78; allegory as parody in, 82–83, 84; CGI, use of, 82–83; commodity exchange in, 84; competition in, 63, 64, 65–66, 68, 72, 80–82; corporate management in, 77–

78, 79, 81–82; domestic modernization and, 45; ending of, 85–86; escape in, 63, 65, 77, 84, 86; family in, 85; as film industry allegory, 79–80; food production in, 66, 79–80, 82; global capitalism in, 65–66; globalization in, 45; global orientation of, 59, 63, 64–65, 80; leadership in, 67–68; logistics in, 66–67, 80; Miramax, Mirando as stand-in for, 79; mirroring in, 81, 83; mise-en-scène of, 77; Monsanto, Mirando as stand-in for, 78–79; pets in, 113; scale in, 23; settings of, 113; simultaneous streaming release, 64; social reproduction in, 66, 84, 85; spatial and temporal dislocation in, 13; translation in, 67, *80*, 80–81, 84; transnational casting of, 58, 64; violence in, 67

Oldboy, 58–59; atemporal juxtaposition in, 61; editing, 60

Olympic Games, Seoul (1988), 15, 32, 112

Parasite (*Kisaengch'ung*), 8; accolades for, 59, 108n24, 111, 129; allegory of, 91; battle royal in, 91, 95–100; box office, 11; class in, 89–90, 108n24; Cold War tropes in, 87, 103; competition in, 87–88, 90–91, 93–94, 96–100, 102; confidence game/*kyehoek* in, 91–96, 99; development of, 122; escape in, 86; fade cuts in, *101*, 101–2; family in, 92, 108n25; gamespace in, 90–91, 92–93, *94*; gamification in, 96, 109n28; globalization and, 86; global orientation of, 59, 65, 86, 95, 102, 103; house allegory in, 73, 86–87, 88–89, 96–97, 102–3; late capitalist sensibility of, 91; mise en abyme in, 86, 92, 103; mise-en-scène of, 5, 23, 24, 32, 73, 86–87, 90, 103; monetary transactions in, 124, 125; nation in, 87; Native American iconography in, 98, 109n30; scale in, 23; set design, 90; spatial and temporal dislocation in, 13, 14, *97*, 97, 101–2; success of, 65, 104, 129; television adaptation of, 115–16; violence in, 89, 98; water and rain in, 106, 116

Park Chan-wook, 16; memory and forgetting in, 58–59
Park Chung-hee, 24
Park Hae-il, 38, 46, 121
Park Kwang-su, 16
Park, Seung-mo, 90
Park So-dam, 92
Park So-young, 14, 115
Park Tae-won, 14, 128–29
parody: globalization and, 68, 83; in *Okja*, 82–83, 84; as translation, 84
pastiche, 84
Pattinson, Robert, 4, 104, *105*, 105
Peppermint Candy, 119
Player, The, 8
police: in *Memories of Murder*, 8, 28, 35–40, 46, 54; in *Mother*, 54, 118
popular culture, Korean, 87, 94

Rear Window, 33
Roh Tae-woo, 107n1

sabaibukei, 96
Sacrifice, The, 117
San Juan, E., Jr., 108n23
scale: in *Barking Dogs Never Bite*, 23, 45; in Bong's films, 23–24
Sea Fog, 128
seo-ri, 21; in *The Host*, 48, 52; IMF bailout as, 50–51
settler colonialism, 87, 98
Seven Samurai, 116
"Shaking Tokyo," 63; development of, 121–22; mise-en-scène of, 42
Shim, Aegyung, 11
Shin, Chi-Yun, 11
Shiri, 16
Siddiqui, Islam, 78
Signal, 36
Smith, Neil, 12
Snowpiercer (*Sŏlgukyŏlch'a*): class in, 10, 105; competition in, 63, 64, 65–66, 68, 72; corporate management in, 71; corporate power in, 82; development and production of, 121–22, 126–27; distribution of, 63, 64–65, 79; domestic modernization and, 45; ecological balance in, 69, 70, 72, 73–74, 77;

Joseph Jonghyun Jeon is a professor of English at the University of California, Irvine. He is the author of *Vicious Circuits: Korea's IMF Cinema and the End of the American Century*.

The University of Illinois Press
is a founding member of the
Association of University Presses.

———————————————

Composed in 10/13 New Caledonia
with Helvetica Neue display
by Lisa Connery
at the University of Illinois Press
Manufactured by Sheridan Books, Inc.

University of Illinois Press
1325 South Oak Street
Champaign, IL 61820–6903
www.press.uillinois.edu